COLLEGIATE

7 BIG IDEAS TO MAKE COLLEGE AWESOME

BY CALEB STEVENS & NICK SALYERS

Editor & Creative Producer: Codie Haddon

Cover Design by: Melissa McDonald, Nick Salyers, and Samuel Moran

Interior Design by: Nick Salyers & Codie Haddon

Printed by: On-Demand Publishing LLC, Charleston, South Carolina

ISBN: 978-1542805568

Printed in the United States of America

10 9 8 7 6 5 4 3 2 1 ...

THIS BOOK IS DEDICATED
TO THE KING. TO MY FAMILY.
AND TO GOOD SHIPS.

NDS

TO MY INCREDIBLE PARENTS:
THANK YOU FOR YOUR LOVE,
ENCOURAGEMENT, AND SACRIFICE
THAT MADE IT POSSIBLE FOR
ME TO ATTEND COLLEGE.

CKS

COLLEGE IS _____.

IF YOU EVER WANT TO SPOT a freshman on the first day of college, find the students who look like they belong on magazine covers with those fresh haircuts and polo shirts.

Never mind the bewildered look on their faces as they traverse the campus bus routes—go straight for the designer labels. That's really all there is to it. You'll be hard-pressed to find anyone who looks better than a freshman on their first day of college. The sunglasses they're wearing are probably new too.

That accurately described my appearance on August 13th, 2012. I (Caleb) had just finished up my first day of college classes. The excitement, fear, and anticipation had been building up to this day for months. It was finally here, and I was ready—new backpack, new haircut, new me!

I was riding on a campus bus that afternoon as I sent a text message to my parents, summing up my day with three simple words:

College is awesome!!!

As far as I could tell, based on what felt like years of experience, it really was. Except for a slight mishap at lunch where I knocked a guy's tray over in the middle of the dining hall. Was it me being a dumb freshman or him not looking where he was going? Hmm… too close to call. Tie goes to the freshman.

For most college students, that text message pretty much captures the first day of school. It's the jam. It's new, fun, and relatively low stress. For a day, at least. ("Syllabus Day" can only be so stressful, right?)

But what comes next? Day 1 of college may be awesome, but what about the next 3.9998 years?

When you walk across the stage at graduation (without tripping, of course), what will you have to look back on? What will it have meant? Will it have been normal or awesome?

We hope it's awesome.

THE BEST FOUR YEARS OF YOUR LIFE?

They say that college is the best four (or five) years of your life. We sincerely hope that's not true. Because if it is, that can only mean two very sad things:

- **A MASSIVE 40-YEAR GAP OF "MEH." PLENTY OF TIME TO PREPARE FOR DEATH AND RETIREMENT!**
- **DAYS FULL OF MEAN BOSSES WHO PROBABLY LISTEN TO NICKLEBACK**

Instead, our hope is that college will be the best four years *yet*. Not the best four years *ever*. An awesome college experience should set you up for an awesome life.

So, that begs the big question: *How do you make college awesome?*

We're glad you asked. That's what this book is about.

A BOOK FROM THE TRENCHES

This isn't a book about developing productive study habits or getting better grades. If that's what you came here looking for, then we've got just the solution. Type "productive study habits" or "how to get better grades" into Google. It's a guaranteed hit.

This isn't a book supported by years of empirical research and hardline data. If that were the case, the title of this book would be completely different. Maybe something like, "On the Nature and Process of the Common University Experience" by Caleb K. Stevens (PhD) and N.D. Salyers (PhD).

This book is different. Two regular college dudes wrote it—straight from the trenches of our real life college experiences. In fact, at the time of this writing, we are both in our final year of college. You read that right. We haven't even officially graduated yet! Technically, we're still in the trenches ourselves.

One thing is for sure, college has been awesome—for both of us—and we want to share with you what we've learned.

WHO'S CALEB?

My name is Caleb. I'm the most awkward person I know. I'm a black-belt level pro at giving side hugs and I once got locked inside a New York subway train all alone in a dark tunnel. I am all about faith, family, creativity, public speaking, and launching big ideas with cool people.

College has been the best four years of my life… so far! Like one long dance party to "Levels" by Avicii. Proudest accomplishment? Winning a lip sync battle to the tune of "Beat It" by Michael Jackson. Thriller jacket, wig, dance moves and all.

Who's Nick?

Hey! I'm Nick. I am a swimmer (but I will probably be a swammer by the time this book comes out). I am a Georgia Bulldawg. I love adventure, traveling, entrepreneurship, and stories.

Some important things you need to know about me are that I got third place in a cutest baby competition when I was born, my personal record for high fives in a minute is 198 (that's 3.3 per second), I once was a hand model for a gas station convenience store, and I've never had a banana chip that I didn't like.

Let's Start Here

Making college awesome begins when we get on board with three core ideas.

1. College can be remarkable.

College is not a holding room. It's not some boring place we have to endure until we can move on to better things or "the real world." College is filled to the brim with opportunity, ripe for friendship, adventure, and impact. It's the proving ground for awesome.

2. Living only for yourself is boring.

Awesome doesn't mean self-centered. We believe the best of life is found when you give it away. In the words of Rick Warren, that doesn't mean, "thinking less of yourself; it is thinking of yourself less."

3. You have more time on your hands than you think.

Most likely, you will never have less responsibility and more flexibility in your life than you do right now. This is the time to try stuff, explore, and learn. Netflix and pizza will be there for you after you graduate. College will not.

7 Big Ideas to Make College Awesome

We believe that every awesome college experience has seven things in common:

1) PURPOSE
2) VISION
3) COMMUNITY
4) GROWTH
5) IMPACT
6) ADVENTURE
7) URGENCY

Each chapter will explore one of these seven big ideas. As you read, chances are you will resonate with some more than others. You may be a baller (shot-caller!) at building *community*, but lacking a clear *vision* for where your college journey is headed. You might have a clear *purpose* for college, but not many fun *adventures* along the way. We want this book to help you embrace all seven big ideas.

Whether you're a freshman with a brand new polo shirt, or a senior on the brink of the "real world," we believe these seven big ideas are game-changers for you as a college student. They are what separate normal from awesome.

At the end of the day (or *book* to be more precise), our hope is that these ideas will help change the way you think about college. Because college is too important to get wrong, and it's too short to squander. Opportunity abounds. But time is ticking.

It's time to make college awesome.

So let's get rolling.

0

BREW THE COFFEE

"YOU LOSE YOUR WAY WHEN YOU LOSE YOUR WHY."

GAIL HYATT

PULLING AN ALL-NIGHTER is never a matter of *if*. It's only a matter of *when*. Every reasonable college student knows this. I (Caleb) learned this first-hand from my good friend, Caleb.

One evening during my sophomore year, as we ate dinner together at one of the dining halls, Caleb had a dilemma. He had a massive Genetics test coming up, and he was debating whether or not to stay up the entire night to study for it.

He's one of the hardest working pre-med students I have ever met. His discipline and study habits are rock solid. He's the classic "responsible" student who is always on time to class, never misses a homework assignment, and usually gets straight A's.

Yet there he was—a Biology major with a work ethic that would put Rocky Balboa to shame—debating whether or not to cram for a test. It was in that moment that I lost all hope of ever meeting a student capable of getting a solid eight hours of sleep each and every night. I realized that sometimes, even the most disciplined students have to adopt a Buddy the Elf strategy and just go for a "full forty minutes."

At the end of our conversation, Caleb and I both knew there was only one solution to his dilemma. He had to go for it. He had to pull the infamous all-nighter. But, if he was going to be successful, he needed some help. He needed fuel to power him through the night. He needed coffee.

Coffee = Fuel

I'm also a guy named Caleb who needs coffee. Coffee is the premium unleaded with Techron™ high-performance goodness that keeps my motor running. For me—and maybe you too—a morning without coffee might as well be a morning spent asleep, because there's not much of a difference. Can you relate?

Coffee has its place in the life of just about every college student around. Even if you don't particularly enjoy it, I'm sure you've been asked the question, "Hey! Wanna hang out and grab coffee sometime soon?" It could have been one of your friends wanting to catch up. Or you've heard it because it's the go-to first date line of every college guy. And it works. Like for real. Who would ever turn down free coffee? Exactly.

But even if coffee isn't your thing, I'm sure you can still relate. Every all-nighter requires a form of caffeine. Something has got to keep you plugging along. Whether it's Red Bull, Five Hour Energy, or shots of straight espresso, everyone needs a little caffeine in their life—especially when it comes to cramming for things like Genetics tests. That's the power and pure awesomeness of coffee.

Coffee is also a metaphor for something far more powerful; it's an illustration for the power of purpose.

Just like a good cup of coffee clears your head and gives you the energy to focus on what's really important, your purpose for college (and life) gives you clarity and direction. Without a clear purpose—a clear answer to the question "Why am I going to college?"—you may spend your four years having fun, but you'll likely look back on that time and wonder what you actually accomplished.

Was the time you spent worth it?

Did it count?

Was it truly awesome?

That's what this chapter is about—the power of purpose, why you need it, and how to reflect on it.

Because here's the deal: A clear purpose is crucial for success in college for two big reasons:

1) COLLEGE IS A BATTLE.
2) COLLEGE IS A RUNWAY.

Your purpose helps you navigate both.

College is a Battle

It's funny how the things we value the most are, more often than not, revealed when our backs are up against the wall—when we're challenged in some way.

That's great though because college is a battle that challenges us in at least four ways: Our beliefs, intentionality, grit, and courage. We'll talk about grit and courage in chapter four, but let's take a look at beliefs and intentionality because they are directly tied to our purpose.

When it comes to our beliefs, I'm not talking about the stereotypical professor who tells a student that their entire worldview is outdated, regressive, or flat-out wrong (though that certainly can happen). I'm talking about the challenge that comes with stepping outside of the environment you grew up in. That's often when we are truly forced to discern what we value the most.

My freshman year, I was faced with questions like: Are my beliefs just a product of my upbringing? Is my faith just a façade? Or is it truly rooted in the core of my identity? These questions are key, because they define everything else in our lives, including our purpose.

College also challenges our intentionality.

"Intentional" means to do something on purpose—it's something you actually *meant* to do. Without getting crystal clear about our intentions and why we're doing things, it's hard to make college worthwhile. Because in college, everything is *your* choice. The days of making friends purely out of being in the same building for eight hours a day is over. It's time to become intentional. It's time to do things on purpose.

A girlfriend won't magically appear next to you on the couch while you crush your roommate in FIFA. Neither will straight A's magically appear on your transcript. If cool stuff happens, it happened because someone made it happen. See how that happens?

COLLEGE IS A RUNWAY

College is the asphalt you race down for a short time before taking off for the rest of your life.

You, right this very moment, are headed down that runway. You're inside the cockpit and the engines have been fired. Where is your destination? The wheels are moving, so now is a good time to start thinking about it.

You see, purpose begins now, not later. Like we said just a few pages ago, college is not a holding room we have to sit in until better things come along. I don't know about you, but I often fall into the trap of believing that I have to put my life's purpose on hold until I "figure everything out."

When I graduate and get a job, then I'll…

When I get married, then I'll…

When I have kids, then I'll…

Sound familiar? You're not alone. College is a transient time for all of us, full of uncertainty about the future.

But here's the thing about purpose: It keeps us stable. Amidst the shifting sands of college, our purpose is the solid rock that we can hold fast to. It keeps us on course towards our destination. The purpose that 22 year-old college me has will be the same when I'm (hopefully) still kickin' it at 82.

Purpose matters today because it will matter forever.

Start with Why

There's a really simple way to boil down what we mean when we talk about purpose. It all comes down to the word *why*.

Leadership expert Simon Sinek makes the case in both his bestselling book and TED Talk that the people who make the biggest difference in the world—the people who truly live with purpose—are the ones with the strongest and most compelling *why*.

He points out that Martin Luther King didn't say "I have a plan." He said "I have a *dream*."

The difference between plans and dreams is one of purpose. Dreams—lofty ideas of what should be in the world—begin in our hearts. They are deeply rooted beliefs that guide our actions and can move other people to action as well. Plans, while important, aren't particularly inspiring or moving. MLK didn't bring 100,000+ Americans to march on Washington because of a detailed plan. He shared with them what he believed, and this vision—this purpose—inspired a nation. MLK didn't share the plan. He shared the *why*.

Just like a cup of coffee keeps us sharp, kick starts our day, and powers us through that all-nighter, your *why* is the engine behind your entire college career. The decisions you make, people you hang out with, ways you spend your time, and the major you pursue eventually all come down to the question, "Why am I going to college?"

It may not sound overly complicated, but it's true. Our *why* influences every aspect of our college career.

Ditch the Latte, Go for the Dark Roast

There are three main types of coffee blends—light, medium, and dark roasts. You can probably guess which is the mildest and strongest, but I'll go ahead and make it easy for you.

Light roast is the mildest. It's smoother but often watered-down, making it harder to taste the coffee bean flavor.

Medium roast is a bit stronger. It's generally what most people order. Because of its popularity, it often goes by the name "house blend."

Finally, there is the vaunted dark roast. It's by far the strongest but can come off as bitter. Brew it with care and you've got a robust, rich, and tasty cup of coffee in your hands. Brew it wrong and you might as well be drinking battery acid.

I have friends who love light roasts and some who won't drink anything but the darkest coffee they can find. But then there's an entirely different group of people altogether. These people don't do coffee. Sure, they may claim they drink it, but they're wrong. They drink coffee-flavored sugar milk. These are the latte and frappuccino people. And for years, I was one of them.

For me, dark roast coffee was an acquired taste. For years and years I was the extra whip, extra sugar, extra whole milk, plus caramel and vanilla flavoring, with sprinkles latte type. "Do you want some coffee with that?" was a question I'd hear often. "Nah, I'm good." I've come a long way since that time. Now, I can manage to get by with black coffee plus a tad bit of creamer.

A friend of mine who loves strong, black coffee once told me that when she puts any sort of cream or sugar in her cup, she begins to feel like she's "not drinking coffee." The extra sweeteners dilute the robust taste of authentic black coffee. In her mind, if the coffee beans are high quality, then there shouldn't be any need for additional sweeteners. She's definitely onto something—why would you try to cover up the essence of what you're drinking?

My mentor, Jeff Norris (no relation to Chuck), former leader of CRU at both the University of Georgia and Alabama, puts it another way; he says that college students oftentimes believe "the external is more important than the internal."

We choose grades over learning. Fans over friends. Hook-ups over real relationships. Instagram filters over authenticity. Late nights we'll never remember over late nights we'll never forget.

Instead of ordering a dark roast, we settle for light roasts and lattes. We chase after the ephemeral rather than the substantial. We go for the creamer before we go for the coffee.

Are you tracking with the metaphor here? A cup of coffee is only as strong as its beans, and our college experience is only as strong as our *why*.

Without a robust internal purpose—a *why* that gives meaning to our college journey—we will not have the proper perspective to face each day with confidence, strength, and wisdom. Instead we'll chase after the creamer—the external—and will find that we come up lacking.

It's crucial to have a dark roast (robust internal purpose), but it's going to take some time and space. We have to brew the coffee.

BREWING THE COFFEE IS A PROCESS

Don't freak out just yet. Purpose is a big idea. It is something that often we don't consider and it's OK to not have the answer right away.

Latte

Fans
Filter
Hook-Up
Never Remember
For Yourself
Grades

VS

Dark Roast

Friends
Authentic
Real Relationship
Never Forget
For others
Learning

It takes time. And space. Sometimes even physical space.

The summer before my final semester in college, I interned with a nonprofit in New York City. As fun and exciting as it was being in the Big Apple, it was often quite draining. Riding home to your apartment each day on the subway with 200 of your closest friends (in proximity, not relation) hoping you put enough deodorant on that morning begins to take a toll on you.

Enter Central Park. The beloved 1.3 square-miles of green space in the midst of the loud and rambunctious concrete jungle. A space where, in some parts, you would never know you're standing smack in the middle of the largest city in the United States. It's wonderful. You can breath fresh air, gather your thoughts, and actually think and reflect. Without that space to breathe, New Yorkers would go nuts. The hustle and bustle of the city will wear you out and spread you thin.

The same can be said for the first week of college. Trade the crowded subways for crowded busses (the routes are just as confusing!) and voila! It's just as overwhelming, like drinking from a firehose. It's too much to take in and process in a single week, or even month. And it begins to wear on you.

You leave your family and hometown.

You part ways with many of your close friends, and are now suddenly in a brand new environment surrounded by scores of randos.

You start a new academic career, with classes that are twice as hard and tests that are often worth half of your entire grade.

Here you are. College. New names. New Faces. New Challenges. New Opportunities. How do you filter through so many new things? How do you avoid FOMO (fear of missing out) but also avoid burnout? Your *why* gives you that framework.

As Jon Acuff says in his book *Start*, we all need some "Central Park" in our life. We need space set aside to think and reflect. Space to consider what really motivates us, honestly asking ourselves the question, "Why am I going to college?"

Just like brewing a fresh cup of coffee, considering your *why* is a process. The water doesn't boil automatically. You have to let the water steep, and then percolate over the coffee beans. You have to be patient. (I can hear it now: "But I have a Keurig! I can brew my coffee in 20 seconds!" Just pretend it's 2005 and roll with it.)

Brewing the coffee takes time and attention. So let's get practical.

LANDING THE PLANE

Have you ever read a book that paints a big picture, but never gets down to the practicality of the idea? It's the worst! Imagine if a pilot knew how to take off and climb to 30,000 feet, but didn't know how to land the plane. Like "Oh well, at least I got you this far. I'm sure you can take it from here!" He wouldn't have a job for multiple reasons.

We don't want this book to leave you hanging in mid-air, so for each chapter we're going to try our best to get this baby on the ground— without crashing. (You're welcome.)

The original title for this chapter was going to be "Reflect on What You Believe In." We think that's the key. Making college awesome starts with considering and reflecting upon what truly matters. Why are you going to college in the first place? Are you sipping a dark roast or a latte?

That means you have to think on it. You have to consider. You have to reflect.

We're not here to tell you exactly what your *why* needs to be, but we are here to say that you need one. Hopefully you've seen that by now. We all live for something, and we encourage you to start with some honest, practical reflection.

Here are some ways to reflect:

MOMENTS OF SOLITUDE

You can't think deeply if you're distracted. Caleb and I (Nick) both had a professor, Dr. Clawson (known affectionately by all her students as Doc C), who started every class with a somewhat strange practice—a moment of silence. A real moment of silence. Sixty whole seconds of quiet. Thirty people running into a room ready for lecture and then stopping everything to be still and say nothing. At first it was difficult and weird—to come into class and just sit there in silence—to be alone with your thoughts, if only just for a minute.

But as we continued to practice these moments of solitude, I began to actually enjoy and appreciate them. They were immensely helpful in resetting my day. Whether you came in busy and stressed or calm and happy, they were a chance to reflect and reset. I always came away from them renewed in some small way.

Through solitude and reflection we are able to untangle the distractions—the busy and trivial things of life that distract us from what is most important. This process allows us to find clarity on our priorities. Solitude is going to look different for every person, but it is important to create space in your day to reflect.

Ask Reflective Questions

Asking great questions can lead to great answers. In this case, asking honest and reflective questions of yourself helps you uncover your *why*.

Questions like…

- What do I care truly care about?
- Where am I finding my significance?
- How do I spend my time, thoughts, and energy when I am alone?

These are some pretty deep questions. Perhaps too deep, you might say. But that's the goal here—digging beneath the surface. Getting all the way down to the bedrock, the fundamental things we build our life and identity upon.

The honest answers to these questions reveal the things that motivate us. And sometimes they show us that we've been chasing the external before the internal. The creamer before the coffee. The lattes instead of the dark roasts.

The Mountains are Calling and I Must Go

Many corporations go on an annual retreat where they get away from all the humdrum of the day-to-day business and ask higher level questions of themselves and of the corporation. This is done to realign the mission and purpose of their organization. But it can also be done on the personal level.

Plan a day or two to just get away and be with yourself. I have a friend who is great about doing this every year. He will find a weekend, typically at the beginning of the school year, and drive to a mountain or trail. He will hike and camp for the weekend just to spend time alone. Just him and his thoughts and prayers. He always comes back refreshed and with a renewed sense of purpose that can keep him going throughout the year, especially when times get busy or difficult. I have always admired his sense of purpose and drive and I know that his personal retreats play a big role in that. So get away. Treat yourself to a personal retreat.

I Get By (with a little help from my friends)

Who knew Ringo Starr had so much wisdom to offer on how to make college awesome? The legendary Beatles drummer is right. You get by with help from your friends. Community plays an essential role in discerning purpose. Sometimes it is in the process of articulating something to someone else that you find out what you truly believe. Friendships and conversations help us process our own thoughts and beliefs. This can play out in many ways, but having a few trusted friends (with whom you can talk about anything) will help you find your purpose and build you up in the process.

Exercise

There is something about pain and discomfort that can cut right through the distraction and busyness of life. As a collegiate swimmer, I spent four hours in the pool almost every day of college. While I definitely don't recommend that for everyone, I am convinced that spending four hours completely immersed in water without any distractions allowed me to find focus. I was able to organize my thoughts, reflect on my day (or the day ahead of me) and even write entire papers in my head while swimming. The only difficult part was getting that paper out of my head and into reality after practice.

Laptops and pools don't always mix well.

It is hard to overemphasize the benefits of exercise. They go way beyond looking good on spring break. In fact, the mental health benefits are just as great—if not greater—than the physical health benefits.

Regardless of your exercise preference—running, swimming, rowing, biking, or something else—do it consistently. Not only will it impact your physical health (i.e. help you get in shape), it will help you fight illness, get quality sleep, and increase your mental health. But ultimately, it will give you the focus and clarity you need to reflect.

THROW YOUR PHONE IN THE OCEAN

Sometimes we need to disconnect from everything to be fully engaged in the present. My friends love to throw around the phrase "disconnect to connect," more as a running joke than anything. But it's true.

Smartphones and laptops serve as tools that make the world better and easier, but they can also be major distractors that disrupt focus. So throw your phone in the ocean (or just put it in airplane mode). I actually think they have done the world an injustice by calling it airplane mode. They should call it "focus mode" instead.

Set aside time each week to throw your phone in the ocean and reflect on what matters most. Mornings in particular are great for this—take a shower, brew a cup of coffee (literally!), and do some reading and phone-free reflection.

WORLD'S BEST CUP OF COFFEE!

The next time you order something at Starbucks, you'll be well-equipped to have a life-changing discussion with your barista on the importance of purpose. Boom.

I (Caleb) now wish I could run up to you and say "You did it! Congratulations!" However, to Buddy the Elf's disappointment, there's no such thing as a perfect cup of coffee. Because no is one perfect.

Nick and I are still brewing. We're still learning. As Christians, we can both say that our faith provides the context for our *why*, and that it has deepened throughout our time in college. But we don't have all the answers, and we haven't "arrived."

The good news is, you and I don't have to wait around until we stumble upon purpose. To quote Jon Acuff again, "Purpose is attracted to motion."

We don't have to wait. We can start brewing now. We can begin living with purpose today, laying the groundwork for making college awesome.

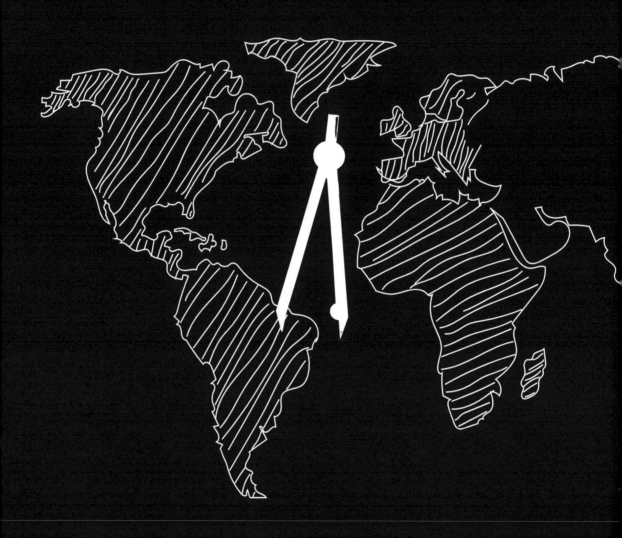

2

CHART THE COURSE

"IF THERE ARE TWO PATHS, I WANT TO BE ON THE ONE THAT LEADS TO AWESOME."

KID PRESIDENT

I (NICK) LOVE THE SCENE from *The Pirates of the Caribbean: At World's End*, where Captain Jack Sparrow escapes from the hands of Lord Beckett. In the private quarters of Beckett's ship, Jack is making a deal with Beckett precisely as the ship is attacked by the Black Pearl. A cannon explodes through the room allowing him to escape his captor and then, with his unmistakable gait, Jack Sparrow strolls about the ship narrowly dodging cannons and splintering wood shrapnel.

He then throws a rope over the ship's upright sail and attaches it to a cannon. In a move of sheer madness, he fires the cannon and the rope propels him up and across the chasm between Beckett's ship and the Black Pearl. As the Black Pearl sails off with Jack Sparrow, Beckett asks one of his officers, "How soon can we have the ship ready to pursue?"

In the background, the mast of the ship topples over due to damage sustained from Jack Sparrow's cannon-propelled escape. The officer then turns back and looks admirably at the Black Pearl sailing away and says, "Do you think he plans it all out, or just makes it up as he goes along?"

What a great line! I can't speak for Jack Sparrow, but I often go through life wondering the same about other people. Does everyone else have a plan, or are they just making it up as they go along?

That is what this chapter is about. Mapping out a vision for college, even if you're not entirely sure where to start. Armed with your dark-roasted robust purpose, it's time to chart a course for what lies ahead.

Too Important to Squander

You need a vision for college because you don't want to waste the days here. College is an incredible time where the responsibilities are minimal and the possibilities are endless. The resources and opportunities that are available to college students coupled with the freedom, independence, and abundance of free time make it unlike any other moment in life.

But without a plan, we can easily squander the amazing opportunities college offers. Does this mean that everything has to be planned and perfect? That there can be no deviations from the charted course? Not at all! There is plenty of room for adjustment and discovery… and even a little bit of making it up as we go along.

But we need a guide, a framework, for how we are going to navigate the high seas of university. We need to have a vision for college.

THE SECRET FORMULA

I have inherited the secret formula for college.

With a line like that, you are probably thinking that Buzzfeed is about to hire me to write clickbait headlines for them. But this isn't clickbait (you already bought the book didn't you?). This is gonna be good.

My dad has discovered the secret to college (and to a remarkable career). Since he is my dad, I convinced him to share the secret with me, so I could pass it along to you, no adoption into the family required. A lot of really smart people worked for a long time to explain what we are going to talk about in this chapter, so focus in.

You ready for it? Here we go: The secret to college is to follow the right triangle. (No, I am not talking about geometry class right triangles. These secret making-college-awesome triangles are more like equilateral or isosceles triangles or something like that. I should have paid more attention in Geometry.)

Ok, that might not sound worth the price of the book just yet, but wait for it—this concept is revolutionary.

To make college awesome, you need a plan—a map to get you

there—and that's what the triangles are. They are the framework that point you towards a destination. A vision that leads you forward.

There are actually a lot of maps out there, a lot of guides to help you find your way through college and through life. But not all of them are good. They don't all lead you somewhere awesome. In fact, most of them lead you straight to a place that you don't want to end up. A place we like to call Normaltown, USA.

Even though it's popular, normal is the enemy of awesome. We have to learn to recognize plans that lead us to normal so we can avoid them. This starts by recognizing what's wrong with the *normal* triangle.

THE NORMAL TRIANGLE

The normal triangle explains how most people approach college, and it goes like this:

- Make good grades (actually, make the *best* grades).
- Build a killer resume.
- Sell yourself to the highest bidder.

The destination of this triangle is to beat all your peers with the highest paying job right out of college. The ultimate goal of this path is to make a lot of money and retire by age 35 (or sooner if you can!).

Normal Triangle

Make Good
Grades

Build Killer
Resume

Sell Yourself to
the Highest Bidder
$$$

Sound familiar?

Now, you may be thinking, "that doesn't sound too bad! What's wrong with retiring by 35? Sounds awesome to me!" And you're halfway right. There's nothing wrong with making a lot of money. But awesome isn't just about the destination, it's about the journey too. Awesome is about the course you are on and how you arrive there.

So, let's look at the subtle flaws in the normal triangle.

First up, grades. Let's get one thing straight (so I don't get in trouble with your parents). Good grades are important! In fact, you should get the best grades you can. But grades can be hollow victories. They should be a reflection of what you learned, but they are often an imperfect measure.

Let me give you an example. Have you ever stayed up all night cramming for a test? (If you haven't yet, I can almost promise you that at some point you will. Make sure to have coffee at the ready.) Despite the fact that you might have missed a class (or seven [Yikes!]), didn't read the book, and only began studying at 9:32 PM the night before, you might have still pulled out a decent grade, maybe even an A. But what if you had to retake that same test six months later? How would you do on it then? Probably not very well.

If you're like me, you crammed all that information in your head, then vomited it all out on the test, got your A, and forgot it all. You didn't actually gain any knowledge. You can get an A on your transcript, and at the end of college even get a diploma, but did you really *learn* anything?

Ok, so what about resumes? Your resume is incredibly important. And you should work hard to develop a strong and compelling resume during your time in college. But focusing exclusively on your resume isn't healthy. The normal way to build a killer resume is to become the president of every club, get a prestigious internship, and volunteer at enough community service opportunities to fill all of the white space available. All of those things are really good. But if you are focused completely on how your resume will read, the words can become empty.

Instead of focusing on building your resume, focus on making an impact. Making an impact is not only going to positively affect the organization you are involved in, but it will also make your resume come alive. Any interviewer will pick apart a resume builder, but an impact maker will shine even brighter *off* of the paper. You will have a stronger case for who you are and what you are capable of. Don't be a resume builder. Be an impact maker.

And last, but not least, selling yourself to the highest bidder. Making money and being successful is great. Aim to work hard and be rewarded for the value you create. However, if the only reason you want to sell yourself to the highest bidder out of college is to retire as soon as possible, then we have a major problem.

Let's say your goal is to retire at age 35. What are you *actually* saying? What that communicates to me is that you want to stop doing what you are doing as quickly as possible (and the sooner the better). That sounds like misery. It sounds like your work has become a prison from which you are desperately trying to escape.

If all you're looking for is a big paycheck and a ticket out of the workforce, you may be missing the whole point.

My dad sure did.

Remember, this secret comes from him. What I've just described as the normal triangle was exactly what my dad planned to do in college. He worked tirelessly at his classes and got straight A's. Every single semester. In every single class. He applied for every leadership role in sight, becoming president of everything he was involved in—and he was involved in everything. His resume was the definition of "killer." Among his graduating class, he received the highest-paying job offer, by a fair margin. And he was tempted to take it until a conversation with one of his mentors changed everything.

In addition to receiving the highest-paying offer in his class, my dad also received the lowest-paying offer. As he wrestled to make a decision about which job to take, he talked with a mentor who gave him this advice:

> *Find a leader you believe in, a company you can be proud to work for, and a role you are good at and passionate about.*

And that conversation changed everything. My dad realized there are more important things than making a ton of money. He realized that being successful financially is not the only qualification for being awesome.

So he took the lowest-paying offer and started working for a humble man who owned a tiny restaurant chain that sold chicken sandwiches. They've grown a little since then; you may have heard of them. The owner was S. Truett Cathy. And the restaurant? Chick-fil-A.

ESCAPING NORMAL

Growing up, my dad shared this story with me on several occasions. He had narrowly escaped an unremarkable and normal career and wanted to make sure I knew the way to avoid normal and find awesome. To be clear, I'm not saying that the path to awesome always follows the ridiculously low paying job offer (still looking out for the parents out there!). But you should use the best map you can find to help you chart your course.

Charting a course towards awesome requires an adjustment. While there are a pile of maps leading to Normaltown, there is one that charts right towards awesome. It's called the *remarkable* triangle.

THE REMARKABLE TRIANGLE

If you want college to be awesome, what should you focus on?

Instead of devoting yourself to making an A, what if you sought out and focused on doing what you are uniquely gifted to do? Those are your talents, and you need to work to uncover them. After you've identified your talents (what you are naturally good at), attain knowledge and build skills on top of those talents, turning them into strengths. Once a strength has been developed, it will help you be successful for the rest of your life. That is not a hollow victory. Strengths are permanent and lasting. You can effectively use them not only six months from now, but even sixty years from now.

Instead of building a killer resume, discover what you are passionate about. A passion is something that energizes you. Something you love. Something that makes you come alive. Something that you could do for hours, and it would only feel like minutes. Passions can be tricky though. Well-intentioned people may tell you to "follow your passions," but that is terrible advice because it is only a half-truth. You should pursue passions that intersect with your strengths.

Remarkable Triangle

Values

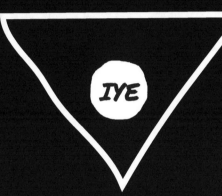

Find your Talents +Skills +Knowledge

IYE

Find your Passions (and your Hobbies)

Find the Job you Never Want to Retire From

Doing something you love but aren't profoundly good at is what we call a hobby.

So how do you differentiate between passions and hobbies? For me, the best example is music. I love music. I love listening to it; in the car, with my friends, as I work, you get the picture. It energizes me. And I cannot help but dance when music comes on, but you would never want me to play an instrument for you, or worse sing. For me, music is a hobby. I love it and I am passionate about it, but I'm not good at it. Making music doesn't fall in my skill-set, so I have found something to do on the weekends and in my freetime (or, in my specific case, the shower), but not as a career.

The last side of the remarkable triangle is this: *Aligned with your values.* This is a very important addition. Our values are the things we hold highest. Life is full of tradeoffs. Each of us constantly makes decisions and swaps this thing for that. Values are what guide us through those tradeoffs. Without clarity on what we value or if we neglect those values in our tradeoffs, our course begins to wander and we end up far away from where we wanted to be.

Combining all of these things—finding something you are passionate about, that falls within your strengths, and is aligned with your values—that's called being "In Your Element" or IYE for short. When you're IYE, you are able to create the maximum amount of value for people in the world. And that's the last filter: Is this something that the world actually needs?

Adding value IYE energizes you. You could not eat for hours and not even realize it; you could pass the whole day and it feels like only a couple of minutes. IYE is where we are able to create the maximum amount of value for the world. Which leads us to the goal of the remarkable triangle: Find the job that you would never want to retire from.

WE WEREN'T MADE FOR THE BEACH

My dad had a few friends who followed the normal triangle. Because they were extremely intelligent and talented, they accomplished the ultimate outcome; they made millions of dollars and retired by age 35 (some of them, sooner than 35), but they were unsatisfied for 10 years of their life in the process.

And guess what happened? They spent about six months on the beach, six months playing golf, and six months at the lake. Before long, they were bored out of their minds. So what did they do?

They went back to work, but this time they didn't follow the normal triangle. They found a job that they were passionate about, that fit their strengths, and aligned with their values. Most of them ended up creating twice as much value in their second career as they did the first time.

We've already met someone in this chapter who lived out the remarkable triangle. His name was S. Truett Cathy. He found the job he never wanted to retire from. He built a $5 billion business from the ground up. As the sole owner, he could have certainly retired if he wanted to. His 401k was fully funded.

But even at the age of 93, Truett was still coming into the office every single week. And if you sat down with him and asked him why, he would respond to you, "Why would I stop doing something that I love so much?"

Isn't that what you want your future career to be like? Isn't that remarkable?

IS THIS JUST SOME THEORY?

When taking a look at a concept like this, I (Caleb) know it can be tempting to write it off as pie-in-the-sky theory. "Yeah that looks great and all *in theory*, but I'm sure real life is way more complicated."

It's true that these triangles are not black and white concepts (even though they're drawn in black and white over there). They are simply a framework to help you go about finding the answers—a helpful way to take an honest look at why you're pursuing the things in front of you. A framework that helps you envision a preferred future.

That's really what vision is—the picture of where you're headed. And it's vision that the remarkable triangle helps bring into focus.

But there are also extremely practical implications for the triangles. I have zero doubt about it. Why? Because I've witnessed it first-hand. It's not just the story of Nick's dad. It's also the story of Allen—one of my roommates and good friends.

HOW ALLEN FOUND HIS CALLING... AND SAVED MY GPA

The trick to increasing your bench-press max is to have a spotter. When you're on your 10th rep and feel like you're pushing a building up a mountain, spotters come in handy. They help you feel like you're only pushing half a building up a mountain. It's a night and day experience. You're able to get more of those "gains" as they say in weightlifting culture.

Throughout college, I normally worked out at the school gym with a friend who would serve as my spotter. But, every now and then, feeling too lazy to actually go to the gym, I'd descend down the stairs into our basement which featured a slightly dusty but reliable weight bench. On those days, my roommate Allen became my spotter.

It was an unusually warm February afternoon in 2015 that I found myself in need of Allen's spotting services. I was on the brink of lifting more than I ever had before, so I was as stoked as a skinny white guy can be.

I looked around the house and found Allen on the back deck talking with Allyson, one of our next-door neighbors. He seemed to be having a serious conversation, so I debated whether or not to interrupt. But this was important stuff! I mean c'mon, I was about to break my all-time record. There was no way I was going to let some "serious conversation" stand in my way, so I asked if he would spot me. After a short hesitation and a thoughtful pause that made it obvious I had indeed interrupted something important, he agreed. (For the record, I hit my record. Turn up!)

Later that day, Allen told me the reason he was a little hesitant to spot me: He was discussing a major decision he had just made. It was similar to a decision that Allyson's boyfriend had also made a few months back, so he was getting her thoughts on it.

Allen was changing his career path. He had been an Accounting major, but decided he was no longer going to pursue a career in accounting. He wanted to do something different. He wanted to teach high school Math.

At first, I thought to myself "that doesn't make sense. How did he ever arrive at that conclusion?" It sounded like going to an ice cream shop and asking to sample *chocolate mocha*. Then after tasting it saying, "I think I want *cotton candy*. Waffle cone, please!" What happened?

Coming into college, Allen had chosen the Accounting route partly because he knew he was gifted at math, but mainly because he felt like that was what he "had to do." If he was good at math and wanted be successful, then of course he should choose Accounting, right? That was the narrative he was hearing in many circles within the business school—the normal triangle.

It went something like this: Get good grades in your so-hard-they-almost-kill-you Accounting classes. Get an internship with a Big Four firm to pad your resume. Then take the CPA exam and go earn the big bucks so you can make it rain!

It was just a few hours earlier on that warm February day that Allen was sitting in one of his upper-level Accounting classes and the thought ran through this head. "What am I doing here? I don't want to do this with my life."

He needed a new course, a new vision. He needed the remarkable way of thinking about college. Deep down, he knew what it was.

During that same semester, we were in a Business Calculus class together. His tutoring was basically the only reason I made it through. One time, he explained a math problem to a mutual friend who then explained it to me in a way that made perfect sense. He taught a concept so clearly that the person could confidently explain it to someone else.

Those experiences began a process of confirming what Allen already knew to be true. He had found his sweet spot. He was in his element, and it was time to pursue it.

When he left his Accounting class that day, he had made his decision. Accounting was now a thing of the past. It was time to follow the remarkable triangle and pursue a career in math education.

Pay close attention to Allen's story. Does it resonate with you? Which triangle have you been following? Which narrative are you listening to? If you find yourself pursuing the normal triangle, it might be time to make a change.

That doesn't always mean changing your major. As a second-semester junior, Allen went on to finish his Accounting degree. But his perspective had changed. He was going to pursue a teaching certificate after he graduated. Allen was moving closer towards the intersection of his strengths, passions, and values.

We're not throwing shade at Accounting majors. We're throwing shade at the *reason* you're pursuing your major. The triangles help reveal our true motivations. In Allen's case, they helped him come to terms with what he felt he was truly called to do.

Chart Your Course

Follow the remarkable triangle. Re-evaluate your vision for college. Turn your talents into strengths. Find your passions (and your hobbies too). And find where your strengths and passions align with your values.

It's going to take some time. You'll probably have a few course corrections along the way. But if you can find that intersection, you'll be on the course to awesome. The course that doesn't try to extract value from other people, but seeks to create as much value as possible.

If you find that place where you are creating maximum value, you will become indispensable to your future organization, and college will be a lot more fun (and by the way, money will never be a problem).

Most importantly, you will have a compelling vision for college. A charted course that leads to awesome things, both in college and beyond.

3

WALK WITH THE WISE

"YOUR FRIENDS WILL
DETERMINE THE DIRECTION
AND QUALITY OF YOUR LIFE."

ANDY STANLEY

SOMETIMES IN LIFE, you just need to have your wrist broken. I (Nick) met John Moore maybe 24 hours before I fractured mine. (For the record, John Moore is just his first name.) If you aren't from Georgia, you need to know that the entire state shuts down at the mere mention of snow, and in January 2011, that was the *only* thing they were talking about on the news. How could I describe my thoughts (or nearly every high school student's thoughts) about a possible snow day? Excited? Jubilant? Elated!? Even the possibility of snow meant a day off of school. But then something happened that didn't occur to us in our wildest dreams… it *actually* snowed! And things. went. crazy. We didn't just get the day off. We got the whole week! And thus began the infamous Snowpocalypse of 2011.

To make a long story shorter, I intentionally stranded myself at my friend's house for the snow week. After the snow started falling, the ice did its due diligence, and school was officially canceled. We began to call all of our friends who were within walking distance (because you can't drive in a GA snowstorm, duh!). It was then that fortune shined upon me. One of our friends had a stowaway at his house too, so they both bundled up and braved the elements to come hang out with us. The stowaway was none other than John Moore.

Over the next few days we played the "board game of our generation": Settlers of Catan, watched hilarious Youtube videos all night and generally had a grand time. Then we decided to go sledding through the neighborhood. We scavenged our garages and basements for anything that would slide (garbage can lids, pool floats, cardboard boxes, you name it) and began searching the suburban streets for the most sled-worthy hill. We were out there for hours, laughing and enjoying ourselves, though only marginally improving our sledding abilities. You see what I learned that day is that it isn't the snow you need to worry about when sledding, it's the ice. Great for speed, terrible for control… and avoiding storm drains. I crashed into a few things that day, but it was *without a doubt* the full-on collision with the concrete storm drain that caused the distal radius fracture in my right wrist.

As I pulled myself out of the snow, not realizing that this crash landing had wounded anything more than my pride, John Moore was laughing and I joined in with him. It was the unlikely start to what would become a great friendship, even though we didn't know it at the time.

The sledding, board games, and fun went on for several more days, and John Moore and I really hit it off. We enjoyed hanging out during the snowstorm, but soon it was time to return to our real homes and get ready to go back to school. John Moore and I probably only saw each other twice over the next two years, but when our high school graduation arrived, we discovered that we were both moving to Athens to attend UGA. Little did I know that breaking my wrist and meeting John Moore would be the way that I would find my core community in college.

Make Moore Friends

Let me tell you about John Moore. He stands out in a crowd. One reason is because he is a gangly six foot six red head. But another reason he stands out is because of his ability to connect with just about anyone. John Moore's sense of humor is lively and weird. He is goofy, fun, and adventurous but also very kind and intentional.

My first Friday in college, I received a text message out of the blue from John Moore inviting me to a party. I told him I would go—not really knowing what to expect. And that was a good thing because I arrived to a scene I never expected. There were hundreds of college students, primarily freshmen, eating barbecue and dancing to electronic music. Being the extrovert that I am it felt like a little slice of heaven. I began to mix and mingle, eat and dance, talk and make friends—not realizing the impact that night would have on the rest of college and the rest of my life.

That night, I met many of the people I would end up sharing the rest of college with. I met people who changed my sense of humor, who would influence my faith, who would show me how to lead, who would teach me what intentionality looks like, and who I would go on grand adventures with. John Moore ended up becoming one of my best friends, and I could literally spend the rest of this chapter telling the stories of our adventures and how he influenced me. I can directly credit so many friendships and cherished memories from college to him. That night was only the beginning.

They say that Rome wasn't built in a day, and my community in college sure didn't form all in one night; it took months and years to be fully built, but the roots began growing that night. I'm convinced that breaking my wrist, meeting John Moore, and going to that party changed the trajectory of my college experience. If I hadn't met those people or been welcomed into that community, my life right now would look very different. That is because your friends have a huge influence on who you are becoming.

Moving and Becoming

There are hundreds of places for you to find your community in college (and you don't even have to break your wrist to do it). No matter where you find it, the community you build will have a powerful influence on the direction and quality of your college experience.

Here's why: *You move toward and become like the people you surround yourself with.*

Let that sink in.

Remember when your dad told you not to hang around with "those kids" on the playground in elementary school? Or your mom used to ask, "if so-and-so jumps off a cliff, are you going to follow them?" You may be chagrined to admit it, but they were right. Hanging out with trouble-makers tends to get you in trouble.

But it actually works both ways. Surround yourself with funny people, and you're likely to start cracking better jokes. Spend time with friends who love movies, and pretty soon, you'll be able to name every Best Motion Picture nominee since 1944. Hang out with a group of runners for long enough, and chances are you'll be running 26.218 miles through a precarious mountain trail in frigid January; and you. will. love. it.

You move toward and become like the people you surround yourself with.

There is a saying that has always stuck with me: *You are the average of the five people you spend the most time with.* College isn't so much about what you are doing as it is about who you are becoming. And who you are becoming is influenced most heavily by the people you surround yourself with. You may have charted a remarkable course—your vision for college may be superb—but without the right community, you will quickly find yourself adrift.

So that's what this chapter is about. Finding your people. Building an

WHAT WE DO < WHO WE ARE
BECOMING

incredible community that will make you better and help you become the person you want to be.

If there is anything worth exploring in college, it is relationship and community. We need it, and college cannot be awesome without it.

COMMUNITY IS VITAL

Here's the thing: We are all *designed* for community. We need and crave companionship and fellowship with other people. It's a quintessential part of being human. This is especially true of extroverted people like me, but even the most introverted people desire and require community too. We all want to be in community. We are hard-wired for it.

Think about the last time you were excited or accomplished something. What was your immediate impulse? Did you want to share that excitement with someone else?

What about the last time you were hurt or sad? Did you want to express your feelings to someone? Did articulating what you were feeling and sharing it with someone else help remedy those feelings?

These impulses reveal the reality that we were not meant to live isolated. There's a reason solitary confinement is one of the most severe forms of punishment used by the criminal justice system! We were not made to go it alone.

Community is also fun—and that's part of the reason we need it. Community is the context for relationships, and relationships are fun and bring us joy—and joy is part of the reason we were designed to be in relationship. Nearly all situations and circumstances are better when shared with others, especially those we love.

But *how*? How do you find your people in college? There are literally thousands of people you could be friends with. Hundreds of clubs and organizations, affiliations, associations, groups, teams, chapters, and circles to choose from. How do you discover *your* community?

FINDING THE CIRCLES

I never knew that my 10th grade Geometry class would be so important. Mr. Free would be disappointed that I can't identify an isosceles triangle or calculate the circumference of a circle, but at least I can make a few metaphors.

Building community is a process of finding your circles. The circles are the groups of people—the friends and organizations and communities—that you belong to. They're *yours* and they can look like whatever you want them to look like.

You will likely have a lot of circles. I mean, you'll probably have more than two, but if you have 71 you should think about scaling back. Some circles may be really big and filled with lots of diverse and interesting people. Other circles may be super small with just a few close friends who share some common interest or experience. The goal here is to find the people who will help you become the person you want to be. Because you *will* move toward and become like the people you surround yourself with.

Finding your circles starts by identifying the areas of your life that are important to you. This doesn't have to be complicated. In fact, it can be as simple as pulling out a piece of paper and making a quick list. When I started college, my "important to me" list looked like this:

- ⧫ FAITH
- ⧫ ATHLETICS (SWIMMING)
- ⧫ ACADEMICS (BUSINESS + MARKETING)
- ⧫ LEADERSHIP
- ⧫ SOCIAL LIFE (FILLED WITH WEIRD AND ADVENTUROUS PEOPLE)

This list begins to tell you where to look for your circles. The reality is that there are *so many circles* that you could be a part of. Take one of the areas from my list as an example: business & marketing. There are diverse majors, business fraternities, internship programs, academic cohorts, professional associations, and certificate tracts all within the area of business & marketing. At first it is a little overwhelming to think of all of the options. Which one is right for you?

But before you get overwhelmed, notice that this list starts eliminating circles too! Since I was interested in business & marketing, I probably wasn't going to find my circle in the Organic Chemistry building. The "important to me" list helps you narrow down your potential circles from "infinity" to something manageable.

One note here before we move on. Your list will likely look completely different than mine! And it should. Your values will help shape your circles. Sure, maybe the big categories might be similar (athletics or social life), but the specifics are likely to be drastically different. That's another key to community. My community isn't yours. And that's ok!

Once you have your short (and probably pretty vague) list, you're ready for the next step: *Actually* finding your circles.

Truth is, finding your circles is more of an art than a science. There isn't some secret formula to it. I wish we could tell you "do these seventeen things and you are sure to find exactly the people you should surround yourself with in college." I wish it were that easy. The reality, however, is much messier.

Finding your circles takes a lot of trial and error and adjustment. It's a process that takes time. And some hard work. I stumbled my way into my community and I bet you are going to do some stumbling of your own. But we want to make it easier for you than it was for us. So that you can stumble a little less and find your circles a little more easily. Here's how.

WHO BEFORE WHAT

To find your circles, you have to focus on WHO, not WHAT. I know we just made a list of *whats*, but hear me out.

It would be easy to take your "important to me" list, run straight to the campus activities fair, and sign up for every organization that has the magic word you are looking for in its title. But if you did that, you would be jumping straight into the deep end and wind up enrolled in nine organizations that might not fit you.

Sure, you would be busy, but community is about *relationship*, not *activity*. That's why it's essential for you to look at WHO first, then figure out WHAT. Just like John Moore led me to the place where the roots of my core community would grow, looking for interesting and challenging people will lead you to circles filled with more people like that.

The best way to explain this is probably to tell you how it worked for me. I came into college knowing that I wanted to surround myself with leaders who had a passion for business. That was definitely going to be an area where I wanted to find a circle. But it seemed like everywhere I looked there was someone or something trying to say that it was the right circle for me. I quickly realized I wasn't going to find my circle by reading club brochures.

Instead, I started paying attention to my classmates and peers. I asked myself who I wanted to become like. Then I looked at the organizations that those people were a part of, and I asked what opportunities they were excited about. I looked at people like Caleb and John Moore. The more I explored, the more incredible people I met. A lot of them were interested in business and planned to apply to a program called the Leonard Leadership Scholars. I took note.

I didn't just look at peers though. I found some people older than me who were doing the kinds of things I eventually wanted to do; people with the kind of character I wanted to emulate. And then, I would go ask them how they got there. For me, there was a guy named Codie Haddon (who is also the editor of this book) and a guy named Michael Lage (who worked for my dad). When I asked them how they got to where they were in business and leadership (similar places to where I wanted to eventually be) they both said that the Leonard Program was a huge part of their development. Duly noted.

So I applied to the program. And it paid off. Standing on the other side, the Leonard Leadership Scholars Program has played a huge role in my personal development, leadership capacity, and has introduced me to some of my closest friends. It became one of my core circles, filled with people who challenge and support me to become the kind of leader I want to be.

So, following the WHO leads you to the WHAT. And eventually you'll start to stumble into your circles and find your place there.

Last note on starting with WHO: Your circles should challenge you and help you grow. That doesn't mean that every time you hang out with your friends you have to be talking about personal development, or how to be more disciplined, or the best new book you've read. But it does mean that, as a rule, your circles should help you become better. So, as Austin Kleon, author of *Steal Like an Artist* (one of my favorite books and a source of the inspiration for this one) says, "If you ever find that you're the most talented person in the room, you need to find another room."

LOOK LEFT AND RIGHT

When finding the circles, the first place to look for WHO is left and right. Look at the people around you: your classmates, friends, and peers. The people who are right alongside you. Who do you admire?

Who impresses you with their character and ambition? Who do you want to become like from among them? Who shares your values? Who shares your interests? Once you've identified those people, you can begin to figure out WHAT.

What are they involved with? What circles are they running in? What organizations occupy their time? Who do they want to become like? This will help you to clarify the kind of person that you want to become and help you to figure out what you might want to get involved in throughout college—what circles might be right for you.

You will continue to look left and right for all of college (and the rest of your life), but you can't only look left and right. There is another key part of finding the circles.

LOOK UP, THEN DOWN

You also have to look up, then down. Just like who, before what, the order matters here too. Up. Then down.

As you find your circles and build community in college, you are identifying the people that you want to move toward and eventually become like. But this can't just be limited to peers; there is only so much someone your age can teach you. To fully take advantage of the circles you are building, you have to look up and identify people above you that you want to become like as well. Look to the people who are older than you.

Looking up could be to someone who is only a year ahead of you in school, or maybe four years ahead of you. It could be a professor or an administrator or a coach. You could look up to a mentor that is in the field that you want to work in one day. Whoever you look up to, find someone that you want to become like, then figure out how they got there.

Take them out for coffee. Pick their brain. Ask them how they got to where they are now. Give them a phone call. And stay connected. It may seem at first like you are imposing on them or their time, but Caleb and I have learned from our mentors that almost all of them *want* to talk with us and help us figure out our collegiate (and post-collegiate) journey. Our mentors have told us that it's fun for them to spend time with us and deeply gratifying.

The key here is patience and persistence. Don't be annoying, but don't be afraid to consistently reach out to them and ask for advice. They may not always be available to you, but your continued pursuit of their wisdom will prove that you value their time and likely incline them to give you more of it. Identifying people who are where you want to be will bring even more clarity to your search for the circles.

The last part to finding your circles is to look down. As you are beginning your quest to find the circles, you might not look down at all. In all honesty, there might not be much to see down there yet. But, as you continue to grow in community and find your circles, looking down becomes more and more important.

Looking down is finding the people below you that you see a little bit of yourself in. It is investing in those girls or guys who are a little bit behind you in the journey. It is giving advice, helping, mentoring, and serving the people who are still trying to find their circles. You are now on the other side. Just as you looked up and found someone that you wanted to become like, now there are people who are looking up to you. Take the time to invest in them. You have enormous potential for impact on their lives.

WISE MAKES WISE

A Hebrew King once wrote, "Whoever walks with the wise becomes wise, but the companion of fools will suffer harm." We've said it a bunch of ways in this chapter, but each variation is getting at the same thing. You give permission to the people you surround yourself with—permission to offer advice on your course, to share dreams and struggles, to laugh and adventure, and (most importantly) to shape who you are becoming. Community matters because it shapes you. You'll either become wise or suffer harm.

There is unbelievable potential in your community as you find your circles. It is not always easy to find community, but it doesn't have to be difficult either. Here are some simple things you can do to make sure you are building a strong (and wise) community.

Ditch Small Talk

Everyone has their typical routine when it comes to making small talk. "How are you doing?" "Good, how are you?" "Good." "How about this weather?" "So this economy… *am I right?*" "That Lady Gaga chick, she is pretty crazy, huh?" Those are a few of my go-tos.

Caleb and I live in the South, and small talk is a big deal. It is just what you do to be cordial and hospitable and nice. I don't know if people just don't know what to talk about with each other or if it is just a bad habit that we all picked up, but Caleb and I think small talk could use a major upgrade.

Instead of asking how someone is doing without really caring about how they are actually doing, ask them what they are excited about. Ask them what has been hard for them this week. Ask them about the last thing that made them smile! We can do so much better than, "How are you doing?" The best part is, the next time you see them you have something to talk to them about and you can escape from the vicious cycle that is small talk.

Second Impressions are More Important than First Impressions

A confidant and good friend of ours has a theory that second impressions are more important than first impressions. You probably understand why first impressions are important, but the importance of second impressions is often overlooked. The second impression is where the precedents are set for the ongoing relationship.

The second time you see someone, are you going to initiate a conversation with them? Are you going to wave to them? Are you going to walk right past them like you don't know them? More often than not, the second impression is going to establish the tone of the relationship that both of you will continue to follow from then on. So make an awesome first impression. And an even better second one.

Ask More Questions. Ask Better Questions.

A great way to build relationships and community is to ask good questions. Asking questions is one of the easiest and most fun ways to get to know someone. It makes people feel cared about and valued—

and can even unlock interesting and awesome things about the other person. Not all questions are created equal though.

Ask good questions that dig below the surface. Ask unexpected questions that induce unexpected answers. Ask fun questions that invite people to share a little piece of who they are.

Questions can show someone that you are *for* them. This intentionality to get to know someone leads to relationships that are deeper and stronger. That is exactly how community is built—through authentic relationships (and good questions).

If you need a head-start on some good questions to ask, check out our question list in the appendix. But if you want the TLDR version, here is my favorite question to ask people:

> **"WHAT IS ONE THING THAT I WOULD NEVER THINK TO ASK YOU, BUT YOU WOULD WANT TO TELL ME ABOUT ANYWAY?"**

I love this question because it gives the other person a blank slate to talk about whatever they really want to talk about. Usually if you give someone the right space to talk or ask the right question, they share with you things they really care about—which leads to even better questions, better conversations, and better relationships.

Live with Fun Roommates

One easy way to build community is to live with fun roommates. Whether you want to or not, you are going to spend some time with your roommate(s). While you don't always have control over who you live with, try to be as intentional as you can be. Most people look at a wide range of factors when deciding on housing, but in my opinion, the thing that should have the most weight in that decision is WHO you are living with, not where you are living (or what you are living in). It is better to be in a miserable place with people that you love than an awesome place all alone. (Then again, that might just be the extrovert in me talking.) Regardless, living with fun roommates is awesome. Don't live with people who are all business all the time. Live with people who are fun.

Don't Get Derailed

Caleb once asked me, "If you could only convey one message to our readers, what would it be?" Without hesitation I responded, *you will move toward and become like those you surround yourself with.* If you take anything away from this book, I hope that is it.

Get community right and you will reap the dividends for years and years to come. Get community wrong and you will face consequences and potentially end up somewhere you never thought you would be.

The biggest obstacle that could derail you from your why or blind your vision is the people you surround yourself with.

Yes, community is hard to build, but it is overwhelmingly worth it. Through community, I found myself challenged and engaged in each and every one of the areas I was interested in. It helped me mature, learn, and grow, but it also supplied the support, encouragement, and fun that community has such a uniquely powerful way of providing. And we want the same thing for you.

Be wise about who you are surrounding yourself with. Your circles will have a huge impact on the person you are becoming.

4

EMBRACE THE HURRICANES

"SOMETIMES WHAT YOU NEED
IS WHAT YOU FIGHT."

SWITCHFOOT

IF YOU'VE EVER HAD A NEAR-DEATH EXPERIENCE, then you're not alone. I (Caleb) almost died once too. At least that's how I felt one cool Spring evening back in 2014 as I stared down at the possibility of death hundreds of feet below me.

"Stayin' Alive" was my theme song that night. I had survived a 200-foot free fall, a 95-foot nosedive, and had hit a top speed of 70 miles per hour. Gulp.

What in the world was I doing, you ask? Surely I was skydiving, right? Or base-jumping? Maybe hang-gliding? You know, something scary and near-deathish.

Uh... none of those, actually. Something waaaaayy cooler!!!

You see, I was at this place called Six Flags Over Georgia. As embarrassing as it is to admit, I had only ridden a "real" roller coaster once before. Prior to that night, roller coasters petrified me.

Imagine how you would feel parachuting out of a military plane into a region controlled by the enemy, missiles and gunfire whizzing through the air as you descended. That was basically how I felt. I was terrified out of my mind, but in a matter of hours, I had ridden every single ride in the park. Whee!

It was 12:01am, the park was closing, and we were on the last ride of the night—Superman. As we taxied up the track, dangling face-down hundreds of feet above ground, it hit me; I actually loved roller coasters. Once I had gotten over the fear of falling out and tumbling down to my death, I was beginning to have fun. Lots of fun, in fact. Something that paralyzed me a couple hours ago had suddenly become the jam.

You've probably heard this story before. Everyone knows that guy or girl who was too afraid to try something new, but once they finally did, they fell in love. Maybe you're like me and you *are* that guy or girl. Aren't we just the worst? We freak out for years and years but once we try, we can't stop talking about it.

This principle applies to far more than roller coasters—especially in college. In fact, it applies to just about every area of our lives.

Any time you step out of your comfort zone in pursuit of something worthwhile, you come face to face with a storm of emotions—typically fear, anxiety, and nervous anticipation.

Let's call these moments *hurricanes*.

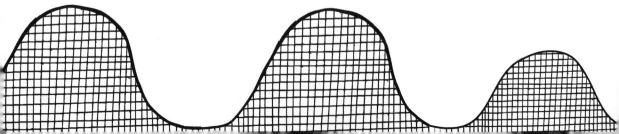

What's a Hurricane?

A hurricane is a moment or experience that challenges you to step out of your comfort zone. It's that thing you know you need to pursue, but frankly are too scared to try. A situation that calls for courage in the face of uncertainty.

In the collegiate sense, it's that nerve wracking thing standing between you and making college awesome. There's no way to get around it. You have to take it head on. I should know, since I coined the term myself! It was all thanks to an experience I had one night on the top of a parking deck… we'll get to that in a minute.

Spotting a Hurricane 101

A *hurricane* is characterized by three things:

1. Hurricanes are unnerving, but not pointless.

There's a difference between a hurricane and a situation that is flat-out foolish. Trying out for the Atlanta Hawks NBA team would be an uncomfortable experience, but for me, it's not a hurricane. Why? Because I'm 6' 0" with a measly 16-inch vertical. It's completely misaligned with my abilities. Leadership expert John Maxwell says "you should stay in your strengths zone, but get out of your comfort zone." It must be uncomfortable, but also aligned with your IYE (In Your Element), as we discussed in chapter 2.

2. Hurricanes require intentional action in the face of uncertainty.

There's a reason why interviewing for a job is more intimidating than ordering a venti size coffee (dark roast, of course) at Starbucks. Or why asking someone on a first date is scarier than asking your roommate what they are doing this weekend. The level of uncertainty is far greater in the first scenarios—and the level of intentionality required is far greater as well. I wasn't going to magically appear on the roller coasters at Six Flags. I had to make an intentional choice to hop on board in the face of fear and uncertainty about the experience.

3. Hurricanes will help you grow.

Whether it's a roller coaster, or a crucial job interview, hurricane situations grow us, regardless of success or failure. When you're challenged beyond the point you think you can go, your comfort zone expands. Certainly success is a good goal, but learning from failure can be just as important and beneficial. Often, we learn more from our enormous failures than from our smashing successes—but only if we see the experience as a valuable learning opportunity.

Either way, you grow when you step out of your comfort zone. And sometimes you discover that failure isn't the worst thing that can

Is this a Hurricane? Checklist ☑

1) Is it uncomfortable? ☐

2) Do I Need to be Here? ☐

3) Does it Require Intentionality? ☐

4) Is the Outcome Uncertain? ☐

5) Will I Grow From this Experience? ☐

happen. Through the hurricane, you gain experience and become better prepared for what lies ahead.

If you find yourself in situations where these three characteristics ring true, chances are you're looking straight at a *hurricane*. Time to embrace it.

HIT THE DECK!

Showing up alone has always terrified me. I don't think it's the showing up part that's the hardest—it's more the fear of not knowing anyone once I arrive.

I'm not a naturally charismatic person when it comes to "mingling." Nick is a pro at it. He's your prototypical extrovert who knows how to "turn it on" and "mingle like a single" and "work the crowd" like it's his job. (I just made up that "mingle like a single" phrase on the spot. Pretty sure it's 100% original. You're welcome.) For me, a sea of unknown faces feels a little bit like a, well, a hurricane.

During my sophomore year, I learned about a group of people who met on top of one of the campus parking decks every week to swing dance. (As you'll learn later, Nick and I *really* like swing dancing). Early in the semester, my roommates and I went to the deck together to check it out. We joined in the dancing and had fun, but mostly hung out with one another.

Several weeks later, I decided I wanted to go back to the deck so I could improve my swing dancing skills, but none of my roommates were up for it (homework or something!). After several minutes of fierce internal debate—I want to dance, but I don't want to go alone—I decided to get in my car and drive to campus.

When I arrived, I began scanning the crowd for one, just one, person who I might know.

Looking… looking… looking… no one.

My heart dropped. My stomach began to churn. I got ready to turn around and drive home.

Maybe you know exactly what that feels like. Maybe you aren't the social butterfly, but more like the introverted eskimo. When you're in that moment, these emotions are as real as category three gale-force winds. But butterflies face hurricanes too. They may look different than the eskimo's hurricanes, but they are just as real.

When you and I come face-to-face with the swirling storm of emotions and fears and discomfort, we have a choice to make: Abort the mission and run for cover, or push into the uncomfortable and see where it goes. Run away, or embrace the hurricane.

(For the record, I stayed at the deck that night, made some new friends, and even picked up a few new swing dancing moves.)

It's Not as Bad as You Think

Embracing the hurricanes is all about getting comfortable with being uncomfortable—in a good way.

Sometimes brewing the coffee means asking brutally honest, reflective questions. That's uncomfortable.

Sometimes charting the course means signing up for a new class or organization in order to build a brand new skill. That's uncomfortable.

Sometimes walking with the wise means showing up to social events by yourself and learning how to meet new people. That's uncomfortable.

I think you get the idea. But here's the kicker—once you jump in and embrace the hurricane, you'll probably realize (like I did on the roller coasters that night) that it is not as bad as you thought it was. The eye of an actual hurricane is calm, and so too are the hurricanes we face in college. From the outside, they look like big, scary storms that we can't handle. But, once we finally jump in, we see them for what really are—intimidating, but manageable. And we grow from the experience.

That's what this chapter is about—learning to grow in the areas that truly matter (whether spiritual, academic, friendship, leadership, you name it). Learning to lean in and embrace the hurricanes so we can become better equipped to make the most of everything college has to offer.

NOT ALL HURRICANES ARE CREATED EQUAL

College is full of hurricanes. Don't believe me? Text your pre-med friend and ask her what she's doing today. While she's responding, I'll go out on a limb and guess that she is studying something difficult. Maybe Cellular Biology or Organic Chemistry. More importantly, she's studying in preparation for a massive test coming up where the class average typically hovers in the high 50s. Yikes. She's about to face a hurricane.

College is filled with all kinds of hurricanes, but not all hurricanes are the same. What you might see as a smooth-sailing-piña-colada-in-hand-Caribbean-cruise might be my version of Captain Jack Sparrow sailing through a violent Maelstrom (Jack Sparrow is one of our heros if you haven't noticed.) Let me explain.

Recently, I was in charge of planning an event, and it required me to find four senior students to speak in front of a crowd of around 300 people. I instantly thought of my super extroverted always-with-people friend, Justin. He's one of the most outgoing people I know, and anytime I see him he is always hanging with friends or rollin' up to social events with his boys (or boyz, whichever you prefer). He'd be a great speaker, right?

If all hurricanes were created equal, then he would be an excellent speaker. But the response text I got from Justin after I had asked him went something like this:

> Hey man! I really appreciate you asking me, but public speaking just isn't my thing. I get super anxious and stuff when I have to speak in front of crowds, haha.

Your hurricane is not necessarily mine. And my Caribbean cruise is not always yours.

For some of us, public speaking feels like being the pallbearer at your own funeral. For others, the thought of interning for a summer in a totally new city is petrifying. Or maybe traveling to a third world country for a mission trip is what frightens you. Maybe it's asking that special someone on a first date. Perhaps it's the brutal three-hour

Accounting or Organic Chemistry test that makes you want to crawl into a hole and hide forever.

Whatever the case, you have to learn to recognize *your* hurricanes.

Because here's the truth—if you are going to make your college career awesome, you cannot avoid the hurricanes. You can't settle for the familiar and the comfortable. You have to lean into the challenge, walking straight into the uncertainty and risk of the unknown. You have to embrace the hurricanes.

WE NEED HURRICANES

Have you ever heard someone say, "Man, what I had for lunch yesterday really challenged me! I learned so much from the experience. Must have been something in the burger!"

L.O.L… of course not. Why?

Because eating a delicious gourmet burger with a pretzel bun and seasoned hand-cut fries is one of the safest (albeit amazing) experiences out there. (Unless you're vegetarian in which case imagine a plate of broccoli sautéed to perfection.) Other than your waistline, you don't grow from eating burgers. It's savory for a few minutes, but beyond that, it's like those chocolate Easter egg bunnies. They taste fantastic on the outside, but on the inside they are completely hollow and lacking in real substance.

We need hurricanes in our lives. If the ocean we're sailing on is always calm, then we're not developing our potential. If we only live for the piña coladas, we miss the fact that there's more to life than our own comfort.

Embracing the hurricanes is necessary for three big reasons:

1. The best of life happens outside of our comfort zone.

Think back on some of your favorite memories or coolest opportunities. My guess is that, at some point, it required a step outside of your realm of familiarity. You introduced yourself to the person who is now your best friend. You interviewed for the summer internship. You signed up for the tough class. You spoke up for what you believe in. You finally hopped on the roller coaster.

Taking frequent trips outside of your comfort zone is *good for you*. Learning to step out amidst the waves is a good thing. It's where new doors are opened, new friendships forged, and opportunities for impact are created. Where's the fun in playing it safe?

2. Sooner or later, we will need grit.

Sometimes, college is just hard. And life can be too. Not all the time, but at some point, you're going to face something that's just plain hard. Maybe it's hard because it's difficult, or hard because it's boring and tedious, or hard because everything seems to be happening all at once.

The solution? Grit—the determination and willpower to stick with it when times get tough.

Grit is crucial because often the circumstance isn't going to get any easier. In these moments, you have to dig in your heels and just work through it. Yeah, the hurricane may beat you up a little, but getting through it is what counts. And what brings the growth.

Grit is what keeps us going. It's not just a word that sounds like an Axe Body Spray flavor; it's a mindset to grind it out and make it through. And it's something you will need for the rest of your life. The good news is that hurricanes don't just require grit, they forge it. Sailing through a hurricane is what builds the grit within you to embrace the next one.

3. We learn how to fail well.

A mentor once told me that I needed to get my failure rate up. At first, it didn't make any sense. How's that for one of those one-line zingers on your resume: "Failing is a strength of mine. Hire me!" I don't think that's what he meant, though. I think he was emphasizing the reality that if you never bother to try, you will never succeed. And if you never fail, you're probably not pushing yourself hard enough.

What's the difference between failing well and failing poorly? The difference comes most notably in what you learn from failure—your perspective on it. Failing doesn't mean *you* are a failure. The late Carnegie Mellon professor Randy Pausch would often say, "Experience is what you get when you didn't get what you wanted." Failing well means learning. And learning means growth.

That is really what all three of these reasons culminate towards: *Growth*. By stepping out of your comfort zone and embracing the hurricanes of college, your comfort zone expands as you continue to sail into new waters.

Put another way, embracing the hurricanes makes you better at life. If the really important stuff in life happens outside of your comfort zone, then the only way to pursue anything worthwhile is to endeavor to take risks.

2 Seconds of Insane Courage

Stepping outside of your comfort zone begins with courage, because courage moves you to action. Without courage, you'll be stuck in place.

Some of the biggest, most influential decisions we make—hurricanes we step into—can be traced back to *2 seconds of insane courage*. A moment when we finally decide to jump.

It takes 2 seconds to…

- Click "send" in your email browser.
- Press the "call" button on your phone.
- Shake someone's hand.
- Jump out of an airplane (with a parachute, of course).
- Step into the interviewer's office.
- Grab hold of the microphone to give your speech.
- Start asking an important question.

All it takes is 2 seconds of insane courage to intentionally choose to put yourself out there. To leap off the cliff into the unknown. To cross the threshold of "no going back." Courage still matters once you leap, but it's the 2 seconds of insane courage that launches you over the edge into the unknown waters.

That naturally begs the question... where does courage come from?

THE ROOT OF COURAGE

Courage begins with your identity—knowing who you are and where your significance comes from. Our identity must precede our actions.

When we live in the reverse order, defining our identity by our actions and performance, things break down. We get stuck on the performance treadmill—the need to constantly prove ourselves to others, fearing rejection and failure. Our lives become emotional roller coasters as we allow success to go to our heads and failure to go to our hearts. We live each day as if we are on trial with the need to justify our case before the jury.

But when our identity is secure, there is freedom to step out amidst the possibility of failure, rejection, and risk, because our worth and significance is not tied to our circumstances or performance. This is where true courage is found.

When U.S. Olympic divers David Boudia and Steele Johnson won the silver medal in the Summer 2016 games in Rio, this is essentially what they said to a reporter who interviewed them immediately after their performance. Their identities were not tied to their medal. They were free to embrace the hurricane of competing on the world's biggest stage. Success could not define them, and failure could not crush them.

What can we learn from David and Steele? They show us that, rather than waiting around until you feel courageous enough to take action, you are free to move forward despite your feelings, because you know that it is neither success nor failure that ultimately defines who you are. You're free to embrace the hurricanes of college and life.

As a Christian, one of my most beloved quotes comes from Justin Clement, the RUF campus minister at UGA.

> **We will either look at our circumstances and come to conclusions about God, or we will look at God and come to conclusions about our circumstances.**

Mic drop.

Start Embracing the Hurricanes

So what now?

Here's a novel idea: Go out and start. I haven't done much research on it, but it seems as if the way to get good at something is to start doing it. Like playing a sport, or creating music, or learning a new subject, or attempting to write a book about college stuff. You just have to start. Like taking the polar plunge in the middle of February. Or back in the day when you finally accepted the ALS Ice Bucket Challenge and became an instant Internet sensation.

It's OK to start small. It counts.

I often fall into the trap of believing that I have to run out of my comfort zone like Aragorn at the end of *Return of the King* as he charges full-on sprint into an army of 10,000 orcs all by himself.

However, we're not talking about putting a man on the moon, or breaking down racial barriers like MLK, or anything else groundbreaking and profound. We're talking about opportunities that exist where you are right now. The hurricanes of daily life.

If it's going to work, you have to make it a daily habit. My dad always says: *Everyday, do one thing that scares you.*

It's as simple as…

- Making the important phone call you've been putting off.
- Answering the dreaded email that's been sitting in your inbox for days.
- Striking up a conversation with that person you see around

campus but have never formally met.

- Reaching out to a mentor and meeting him or her for lunch.
- Applying for the summer job or internship you really want to land.
- Asking a tough or important question to your friend.
- Going to that interesting event on campus, even if it means showing up alone.
- Going to Six Flags and riding all the roller coasters (had to sneak that one in there).

Which of these can you begin doing today?

Start small. Then begin taking bigger steps. Hurricanes are often intimidating, but by resting in an identity that is secure, there is great strength to face the storms of college. Instead of sailing around the storms, we find the courage to sail *through* them.

At the end of each semester, I often review the hurricanes I encountered and write them down. It's always fun to look back on past challenges and see how I overcame them, or what I learned through failure. Overtime, the maelstrom will begin to look like the kiddie pool. The North Shore surfing waves of Oahu start to feel more like something you'd find at Six Flags White Water.

As time goes on, you begin to see real growth. Growth in community, adventure, and impact. But you have to begin somewhere. You have to start embracing the hurricanes.

5

MAKE A RUCKUS

"YOU CAN HAVE AN IMPACT ANYWHERE YOU ARE."

TONY DUNGY

WALTER WAS BORN in a small town in Illinois. As a young kid, he had a knack for art—mostly painting and drawing. Growing up in the early 20th century, Walter drew cartoons for his school's newspaper and took art and photography classes.

At the ripe age of 16, he dropped out of school to join the Army but was rejected due to his young age. He instead joined the Red Cross where he drove an ambulance in France for a year. (Talk about a career change!)

Upon returning from France in 1919, he went back home to pursue a career as a newspaper artist. A few years later, he would team up with his brother and relocate to Southern California, determined to start his own animation company.

They named their very first animated cartoon character *Oswald the Lucky Rabbit*. But as it turned out, Oswald wasn't so lucky. In fact, he was a total disaster, and Walter and his brother soon found themselves completely bankrupt.

But in 1928, everything changed when they created a new animated character—a mouse. His name was Mickey. Perhaps you've heard of him. Walter Elias Disney and his brother Roy were on the brink of forever revolutionizing entertainment and creativity as we know it.

Today, the Walt Disney Company is the second largest media

conglomerate in America. Between its films, TV networks, theme parks, and consumer products (among so many other things) Disney has consistently brought joy to millions of people around the world.

It all began with a young Walt. A man committed to using his gifts in a positive way. A man committed to making a ruckus.

Making a Ruckus

Walt Disney made a ruckus. He used his passion for creativity, his strength in animation, and his values for healthy fun, and brought his ideas to life. It wasn't easy though. It took courage. Walt and his brother Roy both had to embrace some hurricanes: "What if nobody watches our animated films?" "What if people think our ideas are dumb?" "Can our dream become a reality?"

This chapter is about impact—making a ruckus. Courageously utilizing your strengths, passions, and values in a way that meets a need, serves others, and leaves an impact. It's about going for it. Taking a swing. Starting something new. Carrying something forward. Being different—maybe even a little weird. Discovering where you stand out as opposed to where you fit in.

Marketing and leadership expert Seth Godin often uses the term "ruckus" in the business world. Companies like Facebook, Uber,

Apple, Amazon, and Disney have all made a ruckus. They completely changed the ways we connect, get around town, purchase goods, and enjoy entertainment.

Making a ruckus is disruptive. It challenges the status quo. It pushes for positive change and impact, and it's focused on others.

ANYONE CAN MAKE A RUCKUS

You don't have to start a world-changing company to make a ruckus. You can make a ruckus right here, right now. Seth Godin encourages everyone in his or her vocation to make their own ruckus. Regardless of your field, as we'll explore in a minute, everyone has the potential to add value in creative ways. Everyone has something to offer that the world needs. It's only a matter of recognizing that need and courageously stepping forward to bring it to life.

One of the things I (Caleb) love most about college is that it's an amazing place to take a swing at something new. It might be a local band making noise at a concert downtown. Or a college student stepping up and starting a new organization on campus. Or it could be as simple as volunteering your time for a cause you believe in.

Nick and I have observed all of these things and more in our time at UGA, and we've had opportunities to lead some ruckus-making endeavors as well. It's a big reason why you're reading this book. Writing a book can be a scary process. Putting your words out there for the world to read can be intimidating. But truly making a ruckus means you have to be disruptive. You have to break away from the normal way of doing things. You have to lean into big ideas that may get pushback.

Yet it is something that is rarely talked about on campus. Everyone's heard the "make good friends" or "pick the right major" spiel. But few hear "Make an impact. Do hard things." Because, well, it *is* hard. College is often so "me focused" that we forget to look around us, noticing the needs that we can meet with the abilities we have.

But if we never bother to use our talents and passions to serve our university, college can't be awesome. Remember one of the core themes in the introduction: *Living only for yourself is boring.* Living to serve others means making a ruckus. And it isn't boring; it's awesome!

For me, I had to experience it first-hand.

Great Idea + Passionate People + a Basement

Let me paint a picture for you.

Smoke fills the air. The lights are disorienting. I can't lift my arms without bumping into someone. I can feel the bass pounding like thunder, thumping through my entire body. It's loud. I can't hear much. Just chaotic noises amidst terrifyingly loud music. Sweat is running down my face. Most of it isn't mine. My voice is hoarse—nearly gone, in fact. It's been a long, long night, and I'm tired. Actually, exhausted is probably the better word.

But mostly, I'm excited. I'm having the time of my life. I'm grateful for nights like these. And I'll never forget them. Why? Because I'm at a Phi Slam party.

Phi Slam is a student-run organization (independent from the university) dedicated to throwing the best parties at UGA. From crazy raves like the one I just described to swing dance parties to date night socials, Phi Slam has become famous throughout the UGA community for hosting some of the best nights of a college student's life. It's not just partying for partying's sake. It's far more than that.

Don't make any mistake—they party hard. It gets nuts up in there. But it's all for a purpose.

Back in 2005, a UGA student named Chris Odom founded Phi Slam. He had noticed there were few alternatives for freshmen looking to have a good time on the weekends apart from the downtown drinking scene. He founded Phi Slam with the intent of throwing "mind blowing" parties that were alcohol-free. To take the best of a college party—the fun and community—without the risk of negative consequences.

Over the next twelve years, Phi Slam would grow to a leadership team of over 50 students, and would average around 1,300 people at the "big party" they throw each semester. For me and Nick, it played a major role in helping us find community in college.

It all began with a great idea, passionate people, and a basement.

That's the classic story isn't it? Some dude gets his friends together in a basement, and they dream up a world-changing idea that revolutionizes modern life as we know it. Right?

That's what it was like for me during my freshman year when some friends and I launched the ONE2 Conference—not the revolutionize-humanity-as-we-know it part, the four dudes and a basement part.

During the middle of my freshman year, my two senior friends invited me to be a part of an idea they had—a conference for college students centered around the idea of uniting faith and work. As college seniors on the verge of the "real world," they noticed that many of their Christian friends felt as if the only way their lives would matter after graduation is if they went into vocational ministry.

So my two senior friends decided to host an event that paired Christian leaders from all sorts of vocations with college students at roundtables for an evening of conversations about faithful work. It took a tremendous amount of effort to make it happen. From the manpower to build the event space to a team to market and spread the word, it was immensely challenging.

After about a month of breaking our friends' arms (not literally, if I recall correctly) to come to this "random conference thing," we ended up with a turnout of around 80 college students—a number that far exceeded our expectations. What was once a semi-crazy idea being bounced around by a bunch of dudes in a basement was now a tangible reality. And it was making an impact.

As the years went by, we went on to host three more conferences— two in Athens, GA and one in Clemson, SC—with an average attendance of well over 250 people. Watching our team grow from 4 to 30 leaders was an incredible experience. To see people with different skillsets all come together for a common purpose was amazing. It was through the ONE2 Conference that I learned and experienced what it means to make a ruckus.

You Don't Have to Save the World

At this point, it may be easy to say "Yeah Caleb and Nick that's great and stuff, but I'm not entrepreneurial." Or "I don't particularly have a passion for leading a big team of people." That's OK because that's not the heart of making a ruckus. The real idea we're talking about here is *adding value*. Taking your IYE and putting it into action.

Here's the prerequisite: You must be willing to embrace all sorts of hurricanes along the way. That's why the chapter *Embrace the Hurricanes* came before this one. 'Cause we're clever like that.

Making a ruckus isn't easy. It takes courage and a willingness to serve and add value to others. You will need to courageously bring your strengths, passions, and values into your college community. A small ruckus is still a ruckus.

But where do you start? Here's a few questions to help you get going.

1. What gets me fired up?

Electronic dance music, obviously. But what else? What makes you come alive? If you're passionate about something, chances are other people are passionate about that too. Civil Rights activist Howard

Thurman said it best:

> **Don't ask yourself what the world needs; ask yourself what makes you come alive. And then go and do that. Because what the world needs is people who have come alive.**

2. What am I good at?

Passion is important, but like we discussed in chapter 2, it's only part of the equation. Competency matters, too. Make use of your strengths and IYE and put it into action! If you're great at connecting with people, use it! If you can whip a budget together like nobody's business, use it! If you've got a knack for graphic design, use it! Bring your talents, skills, and knowledge to the party.

3. Where do I have influence?

One of the best ways to evaluate your opportunity for making a ruckus is to look around at your spheres of influence. For Nick, it's the swim team. For me, it's my community at RUF—a campus ministry I am involved in. For others, it might be the Biology department, a philanthropy, or a Greek organization. You don't have to start from scratch to make a ruckus. Start with your circles. They are the places where you have influence.

4. What needs to exist that currently doesn't?

At the heart of making a ruckus is this—a need exists and currently it is not being met or at least not adequately. Remember, it doesn't have to be a glaring issue like ending world hunger (though that's certainly a more than worthy cause). My friend started a new Instagram post series for RUF. RUF needed better Instagram posts and, with her creative idea, she made it happen. She found an idea she liked but also met a need. She made a ruckus.

But it would have never happened if she didn't step up to the plate and voice her idea. Which leads us to the last thing required for you to make a ruckus.

PICK YOURSELF

The biggest barrier to making a ruckus is fear. The fear that "this might not work." This idea might flop. People might not show up. They might not care. They might disagree. This book might be lame.

These fears all shout the same thing: *You can't do this. Someone else can do it better. Hold off until you find something you know for certain you can succeed at.*

I love Seth Godin's response. He says "the tiny cost of failure is dwarfed by the huge cost of not trying." He's right. The risk of failure is a prerequisite for doing meaningful work. If we never try new things, we never learn what works and what doesn't work. If we never learn what works, we never succeed.

Don't wait to be picked. If you see a need that you can meet and it aligns with your IYE, pick yourself! Maybe what we're waiting on is you.

RUCKUS
MAKERS

Your ruckus can be anything. Big or small. Elaborate or simple. To further elucidate what I (Nick) mean, here are some awesome examples of how a few of our friends have made a ruckus in college.

TOMMY KEOUGH

Our friend, Tommy Keough, is a landscape architecture major at Georgia. Midway through college, he realized he had a passion and some considerable skill in graphic design. Instead of letting it lay by the wayside, he decided to make a ruckus. He started spending time working on his craft, and found a way to make an impact through his newfound talent. He started a hashtag series called #3wisewords where he showcases "3 wise words" from people in his circles. He creates a beautiful graphic featuring the words and shares it on his Instagram account. It's incredible to see both the response from the community and his development as a designer. Give him a follow at @_tommykeough_ and check out his #3wisewords and you will see what I mean! Tommy is now a fantastic and extremely skilled graphic designer because he decided to add value to those around him and make a ruckus!

CAMERON HARRIS

Another friend, Cameron Harris, is quite an inspiring guy. He realized that although slavery was abolished in the 19th century, slavery still exists in the world today in the forms of human trafficking, forced labor, and bonded labor. He was heartbroken by the fact that there are still over 20 million people trapped in some sort of slavery today, and he had a dream and a passion to help victims of modern day slavery. He started a nonprofit called Breaking the Shackles whose purpose is to raise awareness about human trafficking and to raise funds for organizations who are actively fighting modern day slavery. Cam pursues this mission by hosting a huge benefit concert where all of the proceeds go to organizations engaged in the fight for freedom. They recently raised over $4,500 for Wellspring Living! It has been amazing to see how much the organization has grown under Cam's leadership.

TORRE LAVELLE

Torre Lavelle saw a need in the local community and decided to make a ruckus. She noticed that socioeconomic barriers were preventing young girls from achieving their potential as vibrant, smart, and confident leaders. So she started an organization called Campus Scouts, where UGA students could help start and facilitate Girl Scout troops in the surrounding community. They now have five student-led girl scout troops for low income elementary school aged girls and are moving forward with their vision of helping young girls see and reach their potential. Certainly when you combine green glitter goo, classroom obstacles courses, and selling hundreds of cookies with a troop of rambunctious, singing, dancing, and laughing elementary aged girls, you are going to have a ruckus on your hands!

SHOCKLEY NUNNERY

Shockley Nunnery is one of the most interesting people I have met in college. He is fascinating, brilliant, funny, and headed to Medical School at UVA. He is also a finance major, has interned with a private equity group in Atlanta, and works for a tech startup in his freetime. As if that isn't enough, his story of making a ruckus is equally unique. Shockley discovered that 1 in every 5 kids in America has an undiagnosed eye problem. Many of these undiagnosed eye problems have a major effect on their education. Armed with this knowledge, Shockley set out to make a difference. He constructed a program to help underprivileged kids in both Athens and Atlanta receive free eye screenings. His eye screenings in Athens revealed that 60% of the children they screened had vision problems (much higher than the national average). He was even able to put forth a proposal for the City of Atlanta in which an entire school, where 92% of kids were on free or reduced lunch, was able to receive a free eye screening. Wow!

TREVOR BLESSE

Trevor Blesse is one of my favorite examples of making a ruckus in college. Trevor transferred to Georgia his sophomore year and on a whim picked up a camera to document his year through video. He buckled down and started learning about photography, cinematography, and video-editing. He is completely self-taught, and through the process he discovered he has some serious skill. Trevor has a unique eye and an impeccable sense of creating emotion through video. As he progressed in skill and began sharing his work with the Athens community, people immediately recognized his talent. He is now, in my opinion, the best videographer in Athens and has been hired by several major creative platforms. Trevor changed his career path in the process, and is now pursuing a full-time career in videography as a freelancer. Check out some of his work @trevington on Instagram and check out his vimeo channel, Trevor Blesse.

KATIE WILLIAMS

Finally, our friend Katie Williams decided to make a ruckus in college too. Katie is a leader for YoungLife at UGA, a ministry where college students reach out and mentor middle and high school students. A big part of YoungLife is a summer camp where students have the opportunity to hear about Jesus. But it does require a fee to attend the camp. Katie wanted some of her girls who were unable to afford the fee to be able to go. As a talented artist, she used her passion for painting, drawing, and calligraphy to make it happen. She began creating works of art and selling them through Etsy, as well as doing custom work for her friends. She set aside all of the proceeds from her work to send her girls to YoungLife Summer Camp. Katie made a ruckus and added value to the girls she cares about and believes in.

How to Make a Ruckus

Ruckus-makers come in all shapes and sizes, and they each take different paths on the road to making their ruckus. But what about you? How can you go make a ruckus?

I wish we knew, to tell you the truth. Making a ruckus is a lot like looking at great art. You are not always sure how they did it—Picasso and Da Vinci had vastly different styles—but you know great art when you see it. A ruckus is the same way.

However, there are some common themes that every ruckus-maker embraces. Here's four:

1. Get the right people on the right seats on the bus.

One of my favorite books is *Good to Great* by Jim Collins. (I highly recommend that you read *Good to Great* or, at the bare minimum, the chapter on Level 5 Leadership).

Using a bus as a metaphor, Collins explains what great ruckus-makers must first do: "Get the right people on the bus," and then send the bus in the right direction. Before you set out to impact some place or some thing, make sure you've found some people to come with you. Sound familiar? Your ruckus will only be as strong as the people you bring with you. It doesn't work the other way around. You need to get the right people on your bus and then make sure they are in the "right seats" on the bus—set up to use their skills and passions. They too must be in their "element"—their IYE. The specifics of *what* you do can be clarified later. Great ruckus-makers fill the bus, then steer it.

As you seek to make a ruckus, consider the people on your bus. Are they passionate about the mission? Do they buy-into it? Are they competent in their role? Are they in the right seat?

2. Cast a compelling vision.

Once they have the right people on the bus, great ruckus-makers cast a compelling vision—clearly articulating what they want to accomplish and how they plan to get there. The vision should inspire the people on your bus—those who want to help you reach that vision. A great leader uses vision to answer the "why" of whatever it is they are doing. It helps give their team a purpose.

It is vital to have vision when making a ruckus, especially if you are leading other people. You have to be able to tell them where you are leading them.

3. Lead well.

There is so much that could be said and so much that has been written on the subject of leadership. Suffice it to say this; great ruckus-makers are authentic leaders, and authentic leaders are great servants. They recognize, as Jeremie Kubicek eloquently states, that "Leadership is alive when it is used for others. It dies when it is all about you." In essence, leading well begins with adding value.

Add value to the people you are leading by teaching them, serving them, listening to them, and caring for them. You should believe the best *in* them, want the best *for* them, and also expect the best *from* them. Even when you are not in a de facto leadership role, you can always look for ways to add value to the people around you. Add value to those impacted by you or your organization. Don't extract value. Lead well by creating and adding value. That's what making a ruckus is really all about.

4. Leave a legacy. Build a clock.

Lastly, great ruckus-makers consider the sustainability of their ruckus. They plan to build something that can survive after they are gone. How are you going to leave a legacy? Who is going to keep it going? Again I turn to a metaphor from Jim Collins, this time from his book *Built to Last*. He explains how some leaders are like time-tellers, while some are like clock-builders. Time-tellers tell their companies "what time it is." This works well for a while, but ultimately the time-teller leaves or dies and then the organization can no longer "tell the time." Great leaders are the clock-builders, they spend their time "building a clock" so that even after they leave their organization can continue to tell the time.

This idea is doubly important in college where you are only there for four years. Focus on building a clock so that your ruckus can sustain itself long after you are gone. Surround yourself with leaders and constantly invest in them. One of the signs of a great leader is that their organization does even better after they leave. Not because they were holding the organization back, but because they surrounded themselves with leaders who were even greater than they were. They invested in them so that when it was time to leave, the new leaders took the organization to even greater heights.

Go Make Your Ruckus!

Your university needs your ruckus. You have something—an idea, a spark of originality—that only you can provide. Don't keep it bottled up. Share it.

Put your IYE—your strengths, passions, and values—into action. It will be *awesome*. And you'll be so glad you did.

No one is going to do it for you. Ruckuses don't happen by accident. They are the result of intentional action.

It's time to pick yourself. Go!

6

LEARN TO DANCE

"ONE WAY TO GET THE MOST OUT OF LIFE IS TO LOOK UPON IT AS AN ADVENTURE."

WILLIAM FEATHER

IN ORDER TO FIND ADVENTURE, all you need to do is visit your local grocery store and head for the freezer aisle.

On a seemingly normal Saturday night of my freshman year, a good friend invited me (Nick) to hang out with some people he had just met. As an extroverted freshman, I excitedly accepted the invitation. We decided to get ice cream, so we met up at the local grocery store.

As we tried to make the agonizing decision between Moose Tracks and Chocolate Chip Cookie Dough, the conversation drifted towards the topic of swing dancing. Knowing next to nothing about it, I remained uncharacteristically quiet.

I can't tell you exactly how it happened, but one thing led to another and the next thing I knew, two of the people I had just met, Tyler and Haley, started swing dancing right there in front of the ice cream. What began as a few basic swing moves quickly escalated into a complex, bizarre, and beautiful dance combination that I would later find out is called the candlestick.

Try to picture this: Tyler grabs Haley by the hips and slings her from his left hip to his right. Next she swings between his legs and he tosses her straight up above his head until she is doing a handstand on his shoulders. (I probably don't need to explain now why they call it "the candlestick.")

I almost couldn't believe my eyes. In that instant, standing in the middle of the freezer aisle, I discovered I *had* to learn to dance.

Despite my bewilderment, Tyler and Haley played it off like it was no big deal. We bought a communal tub of ice cream and headed towards campus. On the way, someone mentioned that they knew of a cool hangout spot for us to try. We agreed unanimously to go for it and drove to the building they recommended. We climbed a ladder and enjoyed our ice cream while overlooking campus from (ironically enough) the university's dance building.

With the moonlight above, campus lights below, and a warm late summer breeze filling the air, someone struck up Dancing in the Moonlight on their phone and we began to dance the night away. Admittedly, dance is a loose term as I more stumbled the night away, but the entire experience is one I will never forget. We ended up dancing on the roof into the early hours of the morning, then decided to head back to someone's dorm room and watch one of the best worst movies I have seen in my life (Quarantine 2, if you were wondering).

To me, that night has always felt like the essence of college: making new friends, sharing a tub of ice cream, finding adventure, climbing on rooftops, staying up til completely unreasonable hours, watching horrible movies (and finding people who will watch and laugh at horrible movies with you), and learning to dance.

Adventure is Out There

College is one of the most amazing and unique times in your life. You have more opportunities, resources, and freedoms than you have ever had. You get to share all of those things with hundreds of other people who are exploring the very same adventures.

What do we do with all of those things? How do we avoid wasting or squandering college? How do we take all of these opportunities and turn college into the ultimate adventure?

Start by seizing adventure and then learning to dance!

Adventure Matters

Caleb and I have been talking to you for five chapters on how to make college awesome. Don't miss that. But a huge part of making college awesome is making college fun.

Jon Levy has been studying the "science of adventure" for years and wrote a book all about it called *The 2AM Principle*. He spent a few years traveling the world and experiencing adventure in every country and culture. He came to the conclusion that adventure contains three core elements:

- **THE EXPERIENCE IS REMARKABLE; IT IS SOMETHING WORTH TALKING ABOUT.**
- **THERE IS ADVERSITY OR PERCEIVED RISK.**
- **IT BRINGS ABOUT GROWTH; YOU ARE A DIFFERENT PERSON AT THE END.**

For me, the growth element is the most important. Adventure has the power to change you for the better. It has the power to positively affect you and the people around you.

Adventure is *important*. It shapes who we are and who we are becoming. It can challenge us. It can grow us. It can move us towards others. It stimulates joy within us. It helps us explore. It helps us discover. It helps us push beyond boundaries that we thought impossible. It can help us find meaning, purpose, and passion. And perhaps, most importantly, adventure matters because it is fun!

You and I were made for adventure. That adventure might look very different for different people, but deep down we all crave and desire adventure in our lives. College is one of the greatest opportunities to both satisfy our longing for adventure and discover the adventures we want to pursue for the rest of our lives.

An Attitude of Adventure

The first step in your quest for adventure is to change your perspective. My dad always told me, "How you view things will drive how you do things." The only thing in the world that can immediately change *everything* in the world is your perspective. Read that back over again and think about it for a little bit. Perspective changes everything.

So what is adventure? Is adventure jumping off a cliff or out of an airplane or hiking Mount Everest? It could be. But really, adventure is a perspective. Anyone can choose to have the perspective of adventure in any situation.

Adventure isn't limited to National Parks, overseas vacations, and Instagram posts. Adventure is all around us. That homework assignment, that walk to class, that meal with a friend, that conversation with a roommate, that term paper, that intramural frisbee game; no matter the size, whatever you are doing has the potential to be an adventure. All you have to do is have the right perspective.

A friend once told me that he thought my life was like a movie. While I have had many unique experiences, what he was really recognizing in that moment was my attitude of adventure. I talk to people about the mundane things in my life as if they were grand adventures—because to me they are! (Or at least have the potential to be!)

The Sun Also Rises

One my fondest memories in college was writing a term paper my freshman year. You read that right. Writing a term paper. Scout's honor.

It was a Sunday night, and I knew that I had a paper on Ernest Hemingway's *The Sun Also Rises* due sometime that week. I *thought* the paper was due on Wednesday. You can probably guess where this is going. My roommates and I were about to about to settle in and watch a movie before going to bed. The movie was taking a while to load, so I had about 15 minutes to kill. I thought to myself, "better go check and see when that paper is due." To my horror, the deadline was actually 9am the next morning!!!

Instead of blowing up from stress, I ran to tell my roommates that I wasn't going to be watching the movie with them anymore and then hunkered down in my room and got to work. In that moment, I realized I had two options: This was either going to be a horrible experience or an awesome one; a stressful night or a challenging, yet adventurous journey. It took a little bit of self-convincing, but I chose to view the paper as an adventure.

So, I challenged myself. I said, "I am going to write the greatest paper my professor has ever seen. And I am going to do it all before swim practice tomorrow morning at 5am." It was like a race against the clock. A fight against sleep. A duel with my own creativity. The night was difficult for sure, but when I felt myself drifting into the stress of the moment, I would stop and remind myself to lean into the challenge and adventure.

Around 4am, I finished the paper, got an hour of sleep, and headed to the pool. At 9am, I walked to the professor's office and turned it in. To this day, that paper is the best paper I have ever written. It is the most fun I have ever had writing a paper. And it is the highest grade I have ever received on a paper. None of that would have happened, unless I chose an attitude of adventure.

Your perspective is important. If you want college to be awesome, choosing to have an attitude of adventure is a great start. An attitude full of curiosity, passion, intrigue, whimsy, and possibility. This kind of attitude will keep you in tune with all the potential for adventure that is around you. It might even change the way you view a hurricane.

Most things that are worthwhile require something of you. A risk, some courage, effort, or maybe just straight up hard work. And so, as a rule, the start to almost any awesome adventure or daring destination begins with 2 seconds of insane courage. In addition to being courageous, adventure requires something else: becoming an interesting person.

On Becoming an Interesting Person

If I had a dollar for every time I had to introduce myself in college, I wouldn't be a rich man, but I might have a rOtring 800 or two in my pocket. (For those of you that looked it up, yes a rOtring 800 is a $74 mechanical pencil that is jet-black-weighted-to-perfection-like-a-samurai-sword-awesomeness. Consider sending your favorite author a gift next Christmas???) Almost every single time it has gone something like this… "Name? Nick Salyers. Hometown? Roswell, GA. Major? Marketing. Something interesting about you? …"

That last question, "what is something interesting about you?" can be a daunting question—especially if you are put on the spot. Through the years, it has become one of my favorite questions to answer.

Now before we go on, I need to address something. The rest of this chapter stands on an underlying belief of an adventurous attitude; the idea that *everyone* has value and the potential to be an interesting person.

That is the first step in becoming an interesting person. To believe that you (yes you!) are, in fact, interesting. But it also helps in your pursuit of adventure to believe that everyone has value and the potential to be interesting. If you start to truly believe that

everyone around you has value and vast potential to be interesting, you will be amazed at how many people fit the bill of truly being interesting, amazing, and remarkable. You will be well on your way to experiencing the ultimate adventure of college.

EAT MOR BUGS

On my quest to become an interesting person, I decided to take an Entomology class. Entomology 3300S to be specific. This is not a par-for-the-course class for a marketing major. I took a risk, decided to view it as an adventure, and signed up for it anyway. It ended up being one of the best class decisions I made in college. The most surprising thing is it might have been the best marketing class I have taken in my entire life. Let me explain how that is possible.

ENTO 3300S is a service learning class where we learned all about insects. Then, armed with this knowledge, we would go out into the community to teach other people. Throughout the semester, I taught everyone from four year olds to business professionals to college students to senior citizens—all about bugs! That was a valuable experience in and of itself. But where entomology really connected for me, where I truly came alive, was a concept called entomophagy (yeah, good luck with that one. It's pronounced en-*tuh*-**mof**-uh-gee).

What is entomophagy? I'm so glad you asked! Entomophagy is the study and practice of eating insects. I may have lost you there. What does eating bugs have to do with marketing? The short answer is everything!

How do you convince someone to abandon the instincts they've spent their entire lives developing? That sounds like a great marketing challenge. In fact, it sounds like the greatest marketing challenge of the 21st century! So, that is just what I set out to do.

Every few weeks, our class would oven-bake a bunch of crickets—seasoning them with either parmesan and garlic or preparing them as taco meat. We'd set up a table on one of the main quads of campus with all the proper food preparations: hard and soft tacos, cheese, lettuce, sour cream, etc. I would plant myself behind the table with one job: convince anyone who walked by—student, professor, child, and Athenian alike—to eat the crickets.

One would-be-bug-eater at a time, I honed my pitch until I could convince even the most staunchly opposed to try a crispy, well-seasoned, oven-baked cricket. It took a lot of research and a lot of practice (and a lot of rejection!), but by the end of the semester, for every 100 people who would stop by my pop-up bug kitchen, about 87 of them would try the crickets.

Whenever I get the opportunity (which is more often than one might think), I talk about entomophagy, how it is the future of sustainable food systems, how it solves our water problems, and how great the health benefits are. Through an adventurous attitude, I developed a passion and became more interesting which has led to some really cool stuff.

The Side Effects of Being Interesting

Being an interesting person has a unique side effect of creating an atmosphere of opportunity where other interesting things happen. People are attracted to interesting things. It is like a symbiotic-catalyst that creates a world of possibility. Interesting leads to more interesting. Adventures give way to other adventures.

My junior year in college I was interviewing for a highly selective and highly competitive program in the business school. This program only takes 8 people from the entire business school and they typically take four men and four women. The stakes were high and I needed to find a way to differentiate myself in a 15 minute interview.

Thankfully, the interviewers pitched me a question I could hit out of the park; "What is something in the news that you have been reading about lately?" Without too much hesitation, I replied, "This might be a bit of a curveball, and I am sure that you will not hear this from anyone else that you interview, but I have been reading a lot about eating bugs…" I then proceeded to explain entomophagy and my experience in the class, my sales pitch, and how applicable it was to marketing. Honestly, that is probably the only reason why I got the spot in the program.

While not every new and interesting experience will have a direct correlation to landing a job or buffing up your resume, it will open you up to new perspectives, broaden your horizons, and potentially allow you to find the things you are passionate about. It will help unlock the value that is within you and make you an even more interesting person.

Getting into the Swing of Things

Sometimes adventure is waiting just on the other side of a hurricane. For Caleb and I, one of these adventures was learning to dance. Coming into college I had always enjoyed dance parties like homecoming and prom, but for the most part those were just mosh pits, techno-raves, and the occasional line dance. I was never a skilled dancer, and I even took a test in college which would confirm that I have an extraordinarily average sense of rhythm (important for dancing). But I think more than that, dancing with someone else was something I had no clue how to do. And I was scared of trying.

The risk of standing out—of messing up and looking stupid—was so scary. Not to mention messing up and looking stupid in front of a girl only multiplied the embarrassment factor. Even though I desperately wanted to learn to swing dance, my fear kept me on the sidelines.

In the end, seeing my friends have a blast coupled with the motivating factor of potentially being able to impress that freshman crush and sweep her off her feet with my suave dance moves became so great that I overcame my fear of failure! Luckily for me, swing dancing lessons were very accessible. (This will not always be true for everything, but in college a world of opportunities are available to you and are normally extremely accessible). In this case, there was a group of people that met atop a parking deck (the same one where Caleb learned to embrace the hurricanes!). Every Tuesday night they played swing music and taught swing dancing lessons for free. So I went. I swallowed my pride. I gathered up 2 seconds of insane courage, and I asked to be taught. Then I gathered another 2 seconds of insane courage, grabbed a partner, and we started to learn how to swing dance.

I was not some swing dancing prodigy. In fact I failed a lot at first, but I kept showing up week after week, learning more and failing less. It took some work! Not only did I have to embrace the hurricane of my fear, but I had to keep at it! Often adventure is going to require some grit, some false starts, and some time. There are only a few things in life that you are going to enjoy the first time you do them. Most adventures you'll have to work at, at least a little bit. But it's always worth the effort.

Swing dancing is one of my favorite things to do! I love it! And I love teaching other people how to dance as well. It is something that is adventurous, fun, and adds value to my life and others. (Not to mention it increases my chances of sweeping that special someone off of her feet! Literally!)

Adventure isn't always going to walk up and hit you in the face, but there are ways to open yourself up to opportunities for adventure. Here are a few of our favorite ways to pursue interesting and seek out adventure.

Meet Passionate People...

The easiest way to become more interesting is to surround yourself with interesting people. Their interesting will rub off on you and will help you find things that you are passionate about. In his book, *Blue Like Jazz*, Donald Miller explains it this way:

> *I never liked jazz music because jazz music doesn't resolve. But I was outside the Bagdad Theater in Portland one night when I saw a man playing the saxophone. I stood there for fifteen minutes, and he never opened his eyes.*
>
> *After that I liked jazz music.*
>
> *Sometimes you have to watch somebody love something before you can love it yourself. It is as if they are showing you the way.*

Did you catch that? Passion follows passion. Love creates love. And interesting shows the way to interesting. The lesson is this: Find and talk to passionate people. The more you engage with passionate people about the things they are passionate about, the more you are exposed to that thing, and maybe, just maybe, you'll discover that you are actually interested in it too. At the very least, you will have grown and learned just a little bit more. Your horizons will be broadened.

...Ask Them Good Questions

Explore the adventure of getting to know someone. Asking good questions is a great way to unlock the interesting within yourself and others. Often we leave a lot on the table when we don't take the time or have the intentionality to ask good questions. We pass by most people in life like a ship sailing through icebergs, never taking the time to discover and explore the massive depth that lies underneath the surface. Asking good questions can unlock that submerged depth, lead to adventure, and drive great conversations.

Good questions can also reveal the interesting stories of others. I'm a story junkie. For me, there are few things better than a great story. Sometimes, it takes a great question to draw out an awesome story. You just have to have the courage to ask! Ask thought-provoking questions. Ask trivial, nonsensical questions. Ask well-intentioned questions and questions full of curiosity. You will be surprised by what you learn. And you will be surprised by how much more interesting you become as a result. A great start to being interesting is to be interested.

Ask for Adventure

Ask and you shall receive. Just as questions can unlock awesome stories, questions can unlock awesome opportunities, too. Often, the greatest adventures, the coolest opportunities, start with a simple question.

Not every adventure in life is going to fall into your lap (hopefully by now you know that). But you don't have to wait until life throws you something cool. You can step up and ask for it.

Even small things can start with a question. Ask a friend if they want to catch up over coffee. Ask that person you look up to to mentor you. Ask those friends if they want to go to that local concert later. Whatever it is. Ask good questions. And ask lots of them.

Obviously, we love asking questions. We've compiled some of our favorite questions to ask in a helpful resource at the end of the book. Check the appendix for the full list!

Try Something New

Passionate and interesting people often hide in places that you don't typically go. Good news though. There is an easy way to seek them out. Challenge yourself to try new and different things on a regular basis.

- Go to your college's club fair and play club roulette: download a list of organizations on campus and have a random number generator pick a club for you to try out.
- Find a free night in your week, go to the university calendar and attend any event that is going on that night.
- Show up to that weird local concert.
- Learn a new language or instrument.
- Attend that lecture series.
- Go to a cultural night for a religion or culture that you don't know anything about.
- Bring a friend with you to one of these events (but don't let that hold you back from connecting with new people at the event and fully engaging in whatever it is).
- Take that strange elective class that you want to take. (Caleb and I once took an Organic Gardening class.)
- Go on that study abroad program.
- Meet new people who you don't *think* you share much in common with.

Try something new, even if it's scary or daunting or uncomfortable at first. Maybe try it *because* it is scary or daunting or uncomfortable. Obviously don't abandon your values for the sake of trying something new, but expand your comfort zone a little bit in the right direction. Here's an example.

Literally as I was writing this chapter, my friend, Krystal, invited me to a potluck dinner. The invite both excited and scared me. While I knew the host, I didn't know anyone else who would be there. At first, I honestly didn't want to go. One, because I wouldn't know anyone there and two, because I am not a very good cook. Nonetheless, I showed up with dessert in hand. And showing up made all the difference.

I met so many interesting people. Future investment bankers, an aspiring entrepreneur who tossed around a few business ideas with me, and a girl who took the cake (literally! Just kidding, but she did love the rice krispies treats that I made). She had been to 28 countries, knew 6 languages, worked in military intelligence for 10 years, was missing a toe, and was defending an ax-murderer in court the next week. How crazy is that?! Of course not every person is going to have lived a life like that, but every person has something interesting to share, some value worth noticing. When trying new things, you learn, you meet new (and interesting) people, and you live a life of adventure. Even by going to potluck dinners.

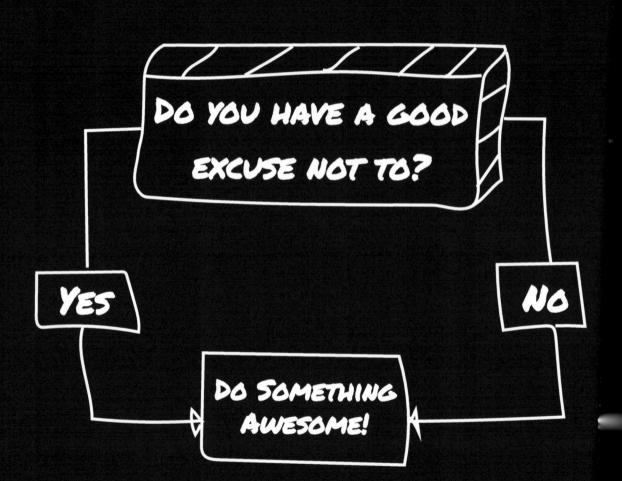

Say Yes

What if I told you that outside of Nelson Mandela passing away, I was the biggest thing to happen in 2013? Well, according to Google, I was. My video was featured in their Year in Review commercial for 2013 (juxtaposed with the late South African revolutionary). This was after it got 38 million views on Youtube, made the front page of Reddit, and was shown on the Today Show and Good Morning America. Celebrities were commenting on the video and America's Got Talent even sent us an email recruiting us for their show. Now what video am I talking about? The UGA Men's Swim & Dive Harlem Shake.

My freshman year of college, a friend and I watched a really weird video on Youtube. It was so weird that we thought it was kind of cool. So we decided to make our own. We were both on the swim team, so we thought it was only fitting for our adaptation to take place underwater with all of our teammates. We messaged everyone on the team telling them to bring a random object to the pool and prepped my GoPro for the shoot. Diving 18 feet down in the diving well, the 25 of us busted some weird dance moves. That night we edited the footage together, posted it on Youtube, and told all of our friends to watch it.

We had no idea we were just ahead of a major trend that was about to sweep the nation. We had no idea that our 30-second video would vault us onto the world stage. We were just a group of guys who decided to say yes. That was all that it took. The rest is history.

I obviously can't promise that you will end up on a Google commercial, but I can guarantee that it won't happen if you decide to say no. Our fifteen-minutes-of-fame-flash-in-the-pan-one-hit-wonder Harlem Shake video is one of my favorite adventures from college. My teammates and I will share the memories of that adventure for the rest of our lives.

And it all started with someone saying yes.

One of my favorite pieces of advice to give to college freshman is this: If you ever have the opportunity to do something awesome or sleep, always do something awesome. You can catch up on your sleep some other time, but you might only get one opportunity at something awesome. Don't get me wrong, sleep is important but don't miss out on an adventure.

If nothing else, say yes. When adventure shows up at your doorstep, don't stay home. Say yes! Say yes when something fun and interesting comes up. Say yes when something potentially uncomfortable comes up. Say yes to adventure. And always say yes to dancing!

7

DON'T WASTE A WEEKEND

"WE DON'T GET TO BE HERE
LONG."

NEEDTOBREATHE

IF YOU'RE EVER WRITING A BOOK about college and find yourself in need of a title for the final chapter, look no further than your friends' Instagram accounts. You'd be surprised at how many of those cleverly worded hashtags are chapter-title material. Such was the case when I (Caleb) was working on this chapter. #dontwasteaweekend

I ~~stole~~ borrowed it from my friend, Austin. He and his wife Katie are recent college graduates, and have since taken their Insta game to a whole new level with this hashtag. Every weekend, they're doing something awesome. Like hiking through the North Georgia mountains. Or taking a day trip down to Savannah. Or road tripping it out west. Or eating delicious food. Every weekend, no matter the circumstance, they make the most of it.

For college students, the weekend is where it's at (or so the story goes). That's where all the "fun" is. The weekdays are what we have to endure to get back to what we truly enjoy. The downtown bar scene. The late nights. The crazy rager parties. The weekend starts each Thursday night and goes all the way through Sunday.

The irony is that these weekends we so often live for are the very moments we end up squandering. Nick once jokingly quipped to me, "At the end of college, no one looks back and wishes they had gotten drunk more." He's right. We've all heard that dude say, "This weekend was so great. I don't even remember it!"

But if college is as great as they say it is—if these are truly some of the best years of your life—why would you want to forget them? Wouldn't you want to make memories and pursue opportunities that you'll never want to forget? With friends you'll never want to forget? At a school you'll never want to forget?

We aren't really the type to go out and get hammered. Maybe you aren't either. Still, there's a temptation to see the weekdays as the grind—the struggle to get by—and the weekends to kick back and enjoy. Instead of going downtown each night, we settle for 15 hours of Netflix and pizza in the friendly confines of our apartment. Turn down for what!

Temptations to squander our time are all over the place. If you are going to make college awesome, you need to recognize two key truths. Two critical characteristics of college. You need to recognize both the *opportunity* and the *urgency*.

RECOGNIZE THE OPPORTUNITY

Opportunity is so baked into the pages of this book, we almost don't feel like we need to address it here. Since you've stuck with us through six chapters, you definitely understand this.

College is unique. Your responsibilities are fairly minimal. There is so much you can do.

College is filled to the brim with *opportunity*. Opportunity to make it awesome. But college won't ever be awesome if you don't believe that it can be. If you're on the lookout for opportunity, you're going to find it.

RECOGNIZE THE URGENCY

You know college is almost over when you get more LinkedIn connections per day than Instagram follows. Or when you're out to eat with your family and the waitress asks if you and your dad are brothers.

(In my head I didn't hear, "Are you brothers?" I heard "You look old and it's time for you to graduate and while you're at it swing by Target to purchase some Just For Men: Touch of Gray." Ouch.)

Take it from us, two guys about to be handed diplomas: College is short. And it never comes back. This is a now-or-never season of life. How are you going to make the most of it? Hopefully by now you have some ideas. Don't wait until your senior year. Start now!

Abby Gets It

My friend Abby is a baller. When I think of people I know who make the most of their time in college, Abby does it better than just about anyone. She's involved with a large on-campus organization, an investment banking society, a highly selective leadership program, a campus ministry, and Greek life.

To top it off, she's a Finance major, which is known for being one of the more challenging majors at UGA. I could go on and on. She would tell you that there are so many other small things that also vie for her time and attention in college. Like SEC football and late night ice cream runs.

And yet, amazingly, Abby is able to do it all. Somehow she fits it all into her schedule and makes it work. Anytime I see her, she's always chipper, joyful, and never comes across as being overly stressed out. It's certainty clear that she has a full plate, but she never seems discouraged or disheartened by her busyness.

I recently invited her to come on my podcast called *Kickin' It with Caleb*. I was curious to hear how she made time for everything. I also thought it would be helpful to share her wisdom with other students. Abby talked about a few tips that have helped her become more productive, but the real secret was in this one sentence she dropped while we were recording the show.

> **I want to look back and know that I made the most of every single moment.**

Dang. That's a powerful statement.

Increasing your productivity and improving your study habits to save time are certainly helpful. Definitely do those things. But, like we said at the very beginning of this book, that's not the real issue.

It's this: College is short. Will you make it awesome? There are a lot of things a Google search can fix, but not this.

At the end of the day, only by recognizing both the *opportunity* and the *urgency* of college can you embrace it for all that it can be. College is shorter than you think. It's also filled to the brim with more opportunities than you can possibly imagine.

That's what this chapter is about. The opportunity to make college awesome, but the reality that time is ticking.

None of these big ideas mean much if you don't approach college with a sense of urgency. A commitment to make the most of every single moment. There's no time to waste. Not a weekend. Not a weekday. Not a single moment.

BE A SAM

Our friend Sam is awesome. He also might be a little crazy. A mutual friend once remarked to Nick and me:

> **I don't know if Sam is just amazingly good at managing his time or if he needs to get professional help.**

I think he was joking, but there was a hint of truth to it. Sam is amazingly driven. He's also amazingly good at managing his time. It's a nonstop thing for him. He's always on the go. Always up to something. All day er' day.

Here's the short list of things he's up to:
- Double majoring in Marketing and Management.
- Pursuing three certificates in New Media, Entrepreneurship, and Leadership.
- Running events for University Union—the largest student events organization on campus.
- Serving as an RA in one of the freshmen dorms.
- Leading university-wide Homecoming festivities.
- Serving as the secretary of his fraternity, BYX.
- Working on the university's yearbook.
- Playing on *two* intramural sports teams.

What do you think? Does he need help or is he just good at what he does? I wasn't sure myself, so one day I decided to ask him. His response was simple.

> **I'm just trying to push myself. I have so many different types of interests, and college is filled with so many opportunities.**

As an RA in one of the freshman dorms, Sam once told me that he often asks his residents the question, "What's something exciting you have coming up?" At first, he was shocked by what he typically heard. "Uh, nothing much."

Really? You're at a school with over 30,000 people, over 600 student organizations, one of the best college towns in the country, and you have *nothing* to be excited about? Nothing? OK.

That's like a tourist going to the Grand Canyon or New York City or Hawaii and saying "Meh, not much to see here." Both Sam and Abby recognize the opportunities all around them. But it doesn't stop there. They take action.

Does Sam have some natural talent? Sure he does. For one thing, he's a second-degree black-belt, a fact I didn't learn until four years into our friendship. But more than anything, Sam goes out all out. Like Abby, he makes the most of every moment.

Sam once asked Nick and me a challenging question: *When was the last time you gave something your all?*

If you're anything like me, you immediately think about two-a-day football practices in high school. Or the morning workouts when they would make you lift weights for over an hour, and then make you run stadiums until you lost your breakfast. (Eventually, I stopped eating breakfast. You can't lose what you never had, right?)

But when it came to my time in college—I'll be honest—I really had to think about it for a minute. When was the last time I gave something my all? Eating burgers and ferociously drinking milkshakes in the dining halls, of course. But what else?

The more I thought about it, I could only pinpoint a few times over the course of, what was then, two and a half years of college that I truly gave everything I had. Times that I was fully spent. Fresh out of energy and willpower. Completely maxed out.

It was a powerful reminder—if something is worth our best effort, why go half-speed? That doesn't mean your calendar has to be constantly booked, as we'll discuss in a second, but it does mean you have to give your best wherever you are. In the classroom or intramural field. On retreat or on a date. Studying or swing dancing. Wherever you are, be all in. Give your all to the things that matter.

Play full out. Be a Sam!

BE INVESTED

There's a common thread that runs throughout all of the remarkable college students we've mentioned in this book—people like Sam, Abby, and the ruckus makers highlighted in chapter 5.

On the surface, you might assume that it's their busyness. And yes, that's certainly true. They are all busy people who probably use those fancy colored-coded Google calendars to help them sort through the madness of their daily schedule. That's not it though. There's something deeper going on here. Something far more substantial.

These are not just busy people, they're *invested* people. And it makes them awesome.

In today's culture, it's easy to confuse the two terms. Being busy is seen as a badge of honor—"I'm busy, therefore I'm important." Being busy can make us feel needed by others, and therefore valuable. Personally, I've got some beef with that narrative.

Even though invested people are often busy people, busy people are not always invested people. In reality, being busy can actually be a roundabout way of hiding from the things we're truly called to do. It really is amazing how busy I get cleaning my room when I have a massive test to study for.

Becoming busier isn't the answer to making the most of every moment in college. While taking action and giving it your all is good, simply filling up your calendar with piles of stuff can be the very thing standing between you and making college awesome.

We don't need *more*. We need *better*.

We don't need a *busy* college life. We need an *invested* one.

And being invested requires at least seven things. (They may look familiar.)

1. It requires *purpose*.

If you're not convinced that what you are doing matters, why give it your best shot? Why even care at all? It's hard to fully invest in something you don't believe in. So consider chapter 1, how strong is your cup of coffee?

2. It requires *vision*.

A purpose without a compelling vision won't take you very far. A ship must know why it is setting sail, but it also must know where it is going. So consider chapter 2, are you following the normal or the remarkable triangle? Have you charted a course towards awesome?

3. It requires *community*.

You can't be fully invested in college without community. You were made for it. It's refreshing and restorative. You will shrivel up without it. So consider chapter 3, because you will become like the people you surround yourself with.

4. It requires *growth*.

Being invested means you expect to see a return on your investment. You believe in it, and expect to see it grow. Real growth happens outside of your comfort zone. So consider chapter 4. Are you growing? What hurricanes do you need to start embracing?

5. It requires *impact*.

Investing means making a ruckus. Shaking things up. Pouring yourself into things that matter. Making a difference in the lives of others. How can you put your IYE (In Your Element) into action and make an impact on your university? Consider chapter 5, how will you make a ruckus within your sphere of influence?

6. It requires *adventure*.

Investing in something doesn't mean "boring" like stocks and bonds. Investing yourself into college means being open to new experiences, ideas, fun, and adventures. Consider chapter 6 and find the freezer aisle where you can learn to dance.

7. And it requires *urgency*. So let's get back to it.

As much as it pains me to admit it as a UGA football fan, I love watching (as of 2016) Auburn's offense. At its best, it's fast and effective. The head coach on the sidelines waves his hand around yelling "Go! Go! Go!" when he wants the offense to speed up even faster. I love that. The football game matters—they're invested in the game and time is ticking. So finally, consider this chapter. Where do you lack a sense of urgency? Where do you need to run the hurry-up offense?

We've said this is a book about making college awesome, and it is. But really, the heart of this book is about being invested. Being all in to go all out. Truly awesome college experiences are invested, and being invested is awesome.

LANDING THE PLANE... ONE LAST TIME!

College is filled to the brim with opportunity and time is ticking. To brew the coffee and live with purpose. To explore your strengths and discover your passions. To embrace the pursuit of authentic, wise community. To step out of your comfort zone. To make a ruckus. And to say yes to adventure.

As we come in for a final landing, we want to leave you with six insanely practical ways to help you make the most of every collegiate moment.

1) JUMP IN! DON'T TIP TOE.

I once heard a friend give some great advice to freshmen entering college. He said, "Don't be afraid to cut ties with your hometown. Seriously. Really lean into your new life here and be all in."

What he's not saying: *Never call your parents and forget about all your high school friends. Don't you dare think about going home even once this semester! Missing your family is for pansies!*

What he is saying: *The sooner you fully jump into this new thing called college, the easier it will be to build community, adjust academically, and establish a solid foundation to make it awesome.*

2) LEARN TO RECOGNIZE THE SEASONS.

Just like the hot-and-humid summer eventually turns into red and orange leaves blowing blissfully in the cool Fall air while you drive with your windows down sipping a Pumpkin Spice Latte listening to Ben Rector, the seasons of college change as well.

You'll experience seasons of intense school pressure on top of an already busy schedule. Yet other seasons will be light on academics, providing the space to invest in relationships.

What season are you currently in? If you have to grind with school, grind. If you have the margin to invest more deeply in friendships, invest. Enjoy the season in front of you, even if it is a crazy busy one.

3) Be where you are, wherever you are.

When I look at college students who have made college awesome, I've noticed they are all pros at being present. No matter what they're doing, they are focused in on what is in front of them. There may be four or five other things competing for their attention, but they don't let that distract from the person or project or party that's right here, right now.

Staying present requires a ton of discipline, but for every ounce of effort you put in, you'll get out even more quality. When you show up, leave everything else behind. You can't be fully present if you're distracted. Whatever is trying to pull you away will still be there when you're done. We promise.

4) Say yes (to the right things) twice as much as you say no.

A mentor once advised me and Nick, "You're in your 20s. Say 'yes' to more than you should for this season of life. Over time, you'll begin to find where your passions and gifts lie and you can focus in on those and say no more often. But for now, say 'yes!'" Make sure your "Yes/No" graph looks something like this:

YES/NO GRAPH

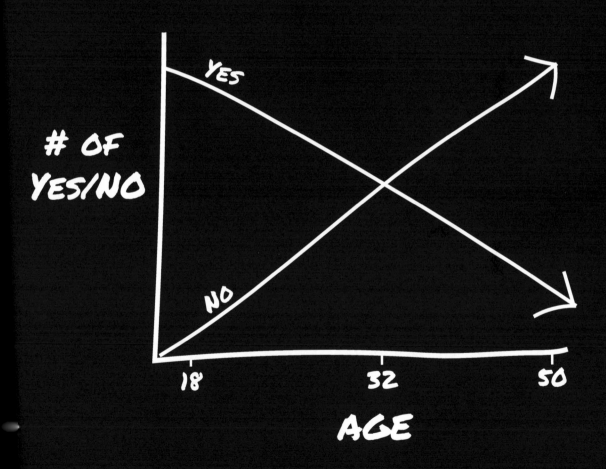

You'll never have less responsibility and more flexibility in your life than you do right now. Now is the time to try stuff, to explore, and to learn. It's how awesome happens.

5) Create space for rest and relaxation.

As you're reading this, it can be easy to think the message is: "Fill your schedule to the brim. Burn all the boats. Never take breaks. Don't have a social life; just go hard and don't stop! Float like a butterfly and sting like a bee!" That's not what we're saying. Not at all.

During our podcast conversation, Abby said one of the ways she creates space for rest is by not doing homework on Sundays. My roommates and I make it a point to get dinner together each Tuesday night at one of the dining halls. Other friends find time on the weekends to go hiking or chill in an eno and take a nap.

Free time—time to kick back, relax, and enjoy yourself (alone or with friends)—is not wasted time. In fact, it's necessary for your GO time to be as awesome as it can be. It won't just happen. You have to create space for it.

6) Have a plan (and be willing to ditch it!).

The great paradox of pursuing awesome in college is that it takes intentional action, but some of the best opportunities show up when you are not looking for them. There's value in both planning and in spontaneity. The trick is to pursue both.

If you're the freshman who had all four years of classes planned out before orientation was over, you probably need to lean into some impromptu adventures with your "less put together" friends (that's planner code for "fly-by-the-seat-of-their-pants"). And if you're the friend who is always suggesting spontaneous road trips or find yourself frequently saying "Let's just try it!" maybe ask your planner friend to show you how to use Google Calendar. It might change your life.

Be intentional with the important stuff: your purpose, your IYE, and your community. But go all in when opportunities and adventures show up.

GOING COLLEGIATE

There's nothing quite like watching your favorite football team run through the banner out onto the field. All of the preparation and hard work culminates into the epic moment as they take the field in front of thousands of screaming fans.

Or when your favorite music artist walks onto the stage to start the show, cameras on and lights flashing. The practice is over. Show time! It's an exhilarating feeling.

Now it's your turn.

We didn't write this book for ourselves. We wrote it for you.

We wrote it because too many people go through college passively. They let the years go by without much rhyme or reason for what college is, and what college can be.

We want you to seize these days. We want your college experience to be unforgettably awesome. We're rooting for you. Now, it's go time.

Go live with purpose. Go chart your remarkable vision. Go build a community worth walking with. Go embrace each and every hurricane that comes your way. Go make a campus-shaking, impact-making ruckus. Go pursue the ultimate adventure. And never, ever, waste a weekend.

Break the banner. Take the stage. Drop the bass.

Go Collegiate.

3, 2, 1...

T THIS!

STUFF WE LIKE...

(AN INTERVIEW YOU DIDN'T ASK FOR...
BY CODIE HADDON)

...COFFEE

What do you order at Starbucks?

Caleb: Grande Dark Roast with room for cream + Iced Lemon Pound Cake

Nick: Not Starbucks. Land of a Thousand Hills. Chemex. Muraho Morning Blend (Medium Roast). Tastes like lemon and rust.

...CLOTHING

What's your favorite shoe to wear?

Caleb: Dark brown leather chukka boot.

Nick: Adidas Original Stan Smiths with gold accents.

What's your go-to outfit?

Nick: Dark, straight-cut jeans, solid color v-neck and a Patagonia nano-puff.

What outfit makes you feel most confident?

Caleb: Well, it's less about what I'm wearing and more about my hygiene. How recently have I showered? When was the last time I got a haircut? Did I spritz cologne this morning?

...CARS

Tell us about your first car.

Caleb: It was a 2003 white Acura TL with a scratch on back bumper that I definitely did not make.

Nick: We called it the Swagger Wagon. Greenish-blueish. 1999 Toyota Sienna Mini-Van. The front window only rolled down (not up), but it had power doors (which was cool when my parents bought it...). I had a permanent playlist exclusively about swagger wagons that played on a loop as I rode around town. The back door was plastered with bumper stickers. My first was also my favorite: "Virginia is for Lovers" (a friend picked it up for me). For senior prom, I convinced all my friends to caravan to the dance. Six min-vans. Eighteen couples. My Swagger Wagon (and our sound track) leading the way.

...BOOKS

What's on the top of your recommended reading list?

Caleb:

- Do Over by Jon Acuff
- The Reason for God by Tim Keller
- Awe by Paul David Tripp
- Befriend by Scott Sauls
- Originals by Adam Grant
- The 21 Irrefutable Laws of Leadership by John Maxwell

Nick:

- Steal Like An Artist by Austin Kleon
- Dawn of Wonder by Jonathan Renshaw
- The Chronicles of Narnia by C.S. Lewis
- The Count of Monte Cristo by Alexandre Dumas
- Let My People Go Surfing by Yvon Chouinard
- Any book ever written by Malcom Gladwell
- The Name of the Wind by Patrick Rothfuss (the best book I've ever read)

...FOOD

Favorite way to cook an egg?

Caleb: Scrambled with salt. Olive oil, no butter.

Nick: Fried over medium.

Typical Waffle House order?

Caleb: Two eggs scrambles, large order of bacon, regular waffle, dark roast coffee with two creams, and a water.

Nick: Grilled chicken biscuit, waffle, and hash browns smothered and covered.

Standard Chick-fil-A meal?

Caleb: Number 3, 12 count with a large fry, and a large, unsweet team with a splash of sweet tea on the top. Plus a frosted lemonade.

Nick: Four count Chick-n-Strips, 12 count nuggets, medium fry, three Chick-fil-A sauce and a lime avocado ranch dressing (the hidden secret of Chick-fil-A sauces) and a lemonade.

Steak?

Caleb: Filet. Cooked medium plus. It's not medium-well, and it's not medium. It's right in the middle.

...DOCUMENTARIES

What do you recommend?

Nick:

- Searching for Sugar Man
- Jiro Dreams of Sushi
- SOMM
- Abstract

...PODCASTS

What do you listen to that we should?

Caleb:
- EntreLeadership
- Timothy Keller Sermons Podcast
- Terry Student Podcast

Nick:
- Revisionist History with Malcom Gladwell
- 99% Invisible
- Song Exploder
- Serial
- How I Built This
- Comedy Bang Bang

...OFFICE SUPPLIES

Favorite office supply?

Caleb: Thumbtacks. I have an awesome bulletin board that I love to pin thank you notes and other keepsakes to.

Nick: The rOtring 800 mechanical pencil....or the cheaper, $10 version called the Draft-o-Matic. It's really solid, but I like it most because it ages well. It looks even cooler after you've used it for around 8 months.

...CANDLE SCENTS

If you were a candle, what would you smell like?

Caleb: Snugly sweater (from Target) or Pumpkin Spice.

Nick: Pine trees and sunscreen and sweat.

...TRAVEL

Where is your favorite place to visit in the US?

Caleb: New York City.

Nick: Either Zion National Park, Bar Harbor Maine, or Seattle.

Where is your favorite place to visit outside the US?

Caleb: Dubai... but I haven't been there yet.

Nick: New Zealand.

...TREES

Do you have an aborial preference?

Caleb: My favorite tree is the Peach Tree, because peaches are dope.

Nick: Why yes I do. I wish people asked me this quesiton more often. My favorite tree is the Western Hemlock. Second favorite is the Southern Live Oak, which just happens to be the state tree of

Georgia.

...*QUOTES*

Share a quote that inspires you.

Caleb:

> *You are becoming today who you will be for eternity.*

Nick: From the prayer of Sir Francis Duke.

> *Disturb us, Lord, to dare more boldly,*
> *To venture on wilder seas*
> *Where storms will show Your mastery;*
> *Where losing sight of land,*
> *We shall find the stars.*
>
> *We ask you to push back*
> *The horizons of our hopes;*
> *And to push back the future*
> *In strength, courage, hope, and love.*

Q

QUESTIONS WE LIKE TO ASK OTHER PEOPLE:

- If you could invite one person who is alive, one person who is dead, and one fictional character to a party, who would they be?

- What is the lamest superpower you can think of?

- What are you an "expert" at?

- What is something small that makes a huge difference?

- What is your guilty pleasure?

- Are you a pancake or a waffle person?

- What is something that you would add to my bucket list?

- What made you laugh today?

- What are you most excited about in the next week? Month? Year?

- What are you learning right now?

- What is your favorite non-citrus fruit?

- If you won the lottery, what is the first gift you would buy for someone else?

- Who inspires you?

- What's your "dream" concert?

- What are you reading right now?

- What are you looking forward to?

- What big thing are you working on?

- What do you know now that you wish you knew then?

- What would the name of your biography be?

- What is a mistake you think everyone should make?

- What is something you wish you had the courage to do?

- What is the most interesting thing you know about but no one else knows exists?

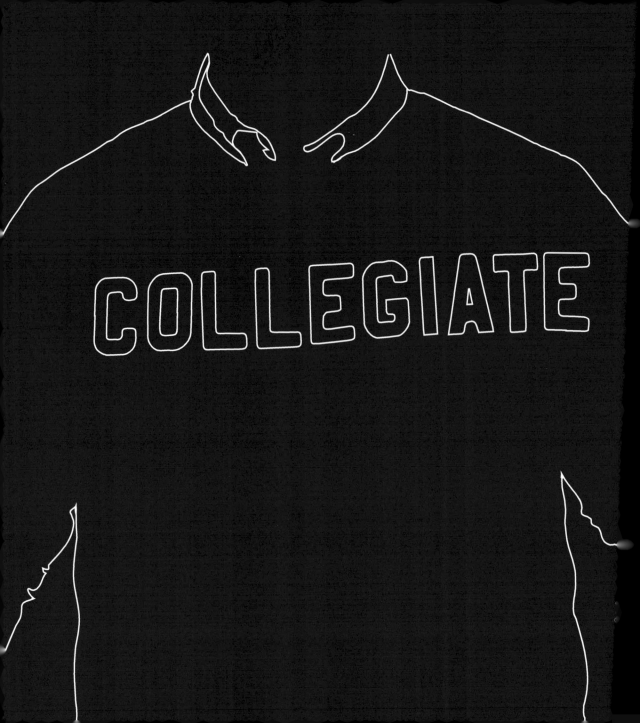

ABOUT THE AUTHORS

Caleb is a 2016 graduate of the University of Georgia where he studied Business Management and Personal & Organizational Leadership. During college, Caleb started a podcast show for the business school, helped launch a faith & work conference, and was the student commencement speaker at graduation. He spent his summers working with startups, independent films, marketing at Chick-fil-A corporate, and the Center for Faith & Work in New York City. He lives just north of Atlanta in Brookhaven, Georgia.

Nick is a 2016 graduate of the University of Georgia where he competed on the varsity swim team while completing a degree in Marketing and certificates in Entrepreneurship and Leadership. Nick has a passion for adventure, community, and stories. In college, he was named a Deer Run Fellow and Leonard Leadership Scholar, and was on UGA's Homecoming Court. He is now the co-founder of Champion Tribes—a start-up in Atlanta that helps fathers and sons connect in life-changing ways.

VISIT WWW.MAKECOLLEGEAWESOME.COM TO LEARN MORE.

Made in the USA
Columbia, SC
14 July 2017